UNMASKING CANDIDATES

Behavioural Inter(nal)view for Recruitment & Selection

I0490477

SREENIDHI S K,
TAY CHINYI HELENA,
ANJALI S. NAIR & FEBY S. JOHN

INDIA · SINGAPORE · MALAYSIA

Notion Press

No.8, 3rd Cross Street, CIT Colony,
Mylapore, Chennai,
Tamil Nadu-600004

First Published by Notion Press 2020
Copyright © Sreenidhi S K, Tay Chinyi Helena,
Anjali S. Nair, Feby S. John 2020
All Rights Reserved.

ISBN 978-1-64828-899-9

Contents

Author's Note

Everyone is very quick to blame the recruiter if he/she makes a wrong hiring decision. They are indebted to listen to what the organization and the selected candidate have to say.

However, has anyone ever given a second thought about what the recruiter goes through, in terms of the problems, situations and the various kinds of applicants that they must face?

Most often, it is very easy to judge someone without knowing their side of the story.

This book provides both the 'Interviewer' and the 'interviewee' an insight into the various facets of the recruiting psychology. It is also a guide for the recruiter to 'hire the right minds', not just the body. So, it is not about the interview per se, but much more about the 'inter(nal) view'.

Acknowledgement

We would like to thank everyone who has been an integral part of providing us with the support and guidance required in the completion of Unmasking Candidates. Special gratitude to Ms. Malavika M for her meaningful contribution in the chapter 'Unmasking Attitudes through Psychometric tools'. We would also like to thank Ms Sudha Suresh, Ms. Stephanie Rebeiro and Mrs. Priyanka Singh for their help in bringing life to the content through a transfer of ideas and the editing process.

We also extend our sincere thanks to Mr. Manoj Pisharody for his contributions.

Chapter 1

Being Better than the Rest

"Good, better, best.
Never let it rest.
Till your good is better
and your better is the best."
- St.Jerome

Most times people are content with what they have and draw a line when it comes to having higher expectations. Only a few would embark on moving from good to better and ultimately becoming the best.

Take the example of Nicole and Suzanne, who have been friends since childhood. Some would call them mirror images of each other and they took pride in it as well. They went to the same school, attended the same university together, scored similar grades and decided to apply to the same company for a job. Nicole was a talker and could convince others to get the job done, while Suzanne would pro-actively do it herself. Both their interviews went well, but only Suzanne got the job. You would ask why, just like Nicole did. It is not because of Suzanne's social status, her last name or anything else. It is because she had the drive to do things in the best possible way and search for a way to make it better.

In a survey conducted across the globe, people were divided into top, good, average and poor performers. The top and good performers think and feel different. They are extraordinary and always put in extra effort in completing their tasks. The quote by Shiv Kera, "Winners don't do different things, but do things differently", fits this situation perfectly. They know how to balance logic and emotional behaviour, and can be sensitive to their emotions as well as others'. Since they can strike a balance between IQ (intelligence) and EQ (emotional), they are whole-brain users. They use the be-do-have technique, i.e., I have to be this, so I'll do this so that I can have this.

The average and poor performers, on the other hand, lack these skills. They function in a have-do-be method. i.e., I have this, so I'll do this and then become this.

What you need to evaluate is if you're just waiting for an opportunity to fall or will you go and seek it for yourself? Which category do you think you fall into?

Develop Yourself and Your Confidence

Dalai Lama says, "With the realization of one's own potential and self-confidence in one's ability, one can build a better world".

While attending an interview, one would often come across questions like "What are your strengths and weaknesses? Where do you see yourself in the next five years?", etc. According to Google, the most common answers include: "I'm a hard worker, but I get tensed if I end up missing a deadline. Also, in five years I see myself in a higher position in your company." These answers have become generic and interviewers are in search of answers that have an element of surprise which can stand out in the pool of generic answers. For this, one needs to first develop oneself and then hone his skills.

Since childhood, you can see parents telling their kids to focus on areas they are weak in. They may be good at English and Music but weak in Mathematics. Special tuitions are always a resort to focus on weaker sides of a student. Why doesn't anyone tell the child that he/she is good in English and should revise it regularly or that he should practice singing daily? Focusing our energies on what we call our weaknesses or areas of improvement is something we always tend to do. This can be attributed to the age-old practice that is followed in our society by our forefathers and been passed onto us from generations.

We should be the torch bearers of tomorrow guided by rationality, focusing on our powers rather than our weaknesses. It is these strengths that help us grow and make us stand out in the crowd and put us in a position that is greater than the others. Who wouldn't want that?

Interviewer's Perspective

While it is imperative to deal with the interviewee's side of the matter, the book closely serves as a guide to the interviewers on how to unmask candidates and understand them better before hiring.

During an interview, it is required that the interviewer should be more attentive than the interviewee. One must pay attention to the details and search for all the qualities that they expect in a potential candidate. There could be circumstances where the requirement is not completely understood and therefore, they get carried away in the direction as projected by the candidate. In situations like these, there are high chances that:

There is inadequate information about the candidate even after a great interview.

There could be assumptions made about the candidate that could lead to hiring or non-hiring.

There exists a dilemma as to whom to hire between two shortlisted candidates.

Frustration due to the time-consuming process.

There aren't enough questions to ask.

Every interviewer would have experienced any one of these scenarios at least once. Let us consider two examples:

Example 1: John was interviewing a candidate for the post of an assistant sales manager at their company. The candidate was very good at structuring her conversations and was a good communicator as well. She could talk for hours and still have the other person's full attention. Considering the fact that every interviewee was given a stipulated time frame and the fact that she was a storyteller, John found it difficult to gather quality information about her even after an hour.

Example 2: The resume of a candidate indicated that he quit his previous job in a span of three months. In nine years, this was his seventh job. This fact was enough to generate quick conclusions among the people who received his resume. However, it is important to know the story from the other side before coming to quick conclusions. He may have had strong reasons to support the information.

Both the situations above have a different way of being dealt, which will be addressed in the following chapters.

Research by LinkedIn has proven that more than 75% of job seekers research about a company's reputation and employer brand before applying.

Chapter 2

Interviewers!!! Be Prepared

When it comes to interviews, the duty to come prepared isn't just that of the interviewee but also of the interviewer. Like the candidate does proper research about the company he wants to join, it is equally important for the interviewer to go through the submitted resume thoroughly. Good preparation takes time, but it also pays off. The interviewer will be able to evaluate the candidates effectively and create a positive environment for the candidate. However, there are certain mistakes that can happen during these processes, which include:

a. Not receiving candidates properly: Most candidates tend to come for an interview eager and on time. So, it is a basic courtesy for the interviewer also to be on time for the interview. Showing up half-an-hour late reflects badly on the interviewer and therefore the company as well. Welcome your candidate—not doing so could demotivate them and affect their performance in the interview.

b. Not reading resumes: Candidates send in their resumes way before the interviews are scheduled. So, it is necessary for the interviewer to go through the resume before the scheduled interview with the candidate. If not, one risks asking questions that are irrelevant and a waste of time.

c. Being distracted: Candidates spend a lot of time preparing for their interview and deserve to be heard. There could be any number of reasons why an interviewer maybe distracted—an upcoming meeting or an important email. If the interviewer does not seem focused during an interview process, they would immediately know and be disheartened, which would affect the interview.

d. Dominating the discussion: Breaking the ice, talking about the company and the way it functions is all part of the interview process. However, an interviewer should keep in mind the fact that it should never take the shape of an endless monologue. Candidates should be allowed to talk, and one should avoid interrupting them frequently. It should also be noted that the scenario if reversed, may also not have the desired outcome. Remaining quiet and only letting the candidate talk without participating in it reflects badly. Therefore, one needs to maintain a balance in the conversation that takes place.

e. Asking irrelevant questions: Asking too many questions that are rhetorical, predictable or irrelevant is not the ideal choice during an interview.

f. Boasting: it is a common tendency for the interviewer to talk about the company; however, one must be careful about being carried away. Boasting about the company and exaggerating it is not something that candidates need to listen to.

g. Dodging questions: In some cases, interviewers could be asked questions they do not have the answer to. It is normal to not know the answers to everything; however, one should never deflect them condescendingly. This is when you tell them you don't know the answer to the question and that you'll get back with the answer or rather direct them to someone who would know the answer to the question.

h. Rushing the process: Candidates are usually allotted a stimulated time for their interview. Sometimes, interviews tend to get cut short due to several reasons. This could affect the performance of the candidate and would result in not receiving adequate data.

i. Revealing too much: The most common mistakes made by interviewers are giving up too much information about the qualities they look for in an individual that will match the culture of the organization. This could become dangerous as it gives the candidates an idea about what qualities to display and enables them to manipulate their answers accordingly. If you really want to speak about the idealistic behaviours that differentiate your organization from the rest, it is best to save it until the end.

Candidates are Prepared to Take You On

For most interviews, the applicants are well-prepared and expectant of the process. Therefore, they tend to selectively respond to questions asked and may or may not be entirely honest. This could lead to the interviewer believing that their stated behaviour is actual actions that they will witness in the future.

These employees slowly start to resemble the rat in the maze who takes effort for the food at the end of it. Here it is the "pay-check" at the end of the month that keeps them running the corporate maze. They may put effort in doing something but will do so with increasing resentment, complaints and passive resistance. They then turn into a liability with no desire for growth and see goals as nothing but forced choices unrelated to their underlying dreams, hopes and ambitions.

In short, Rat-in-the-Maze employees = Liabilities!!

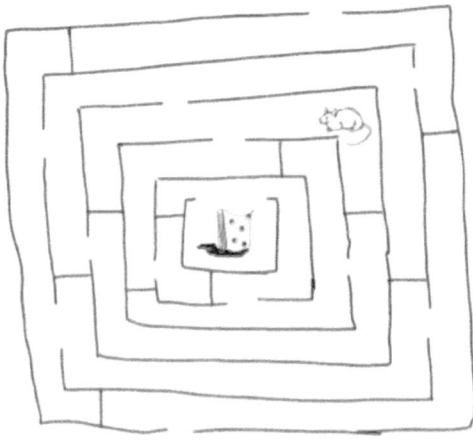

However, the present scenario is slightly changing and not all rats want food at the end. The purpose of every candidate applying for the post may vary. While majority of them need jobs, there exists a few who do not fall into this category. There could be people who think that the job at hand has become monotonous and require a break to explore other areas or better possibilities in their own market. Some would want to know what the job market is, and a few might not even consider their job as the priority. There are also instances where the interviewees just want the entire feel or experience of an interview to prepare for a more important one, while others are just desperate for a job. No one can determine the reasons and intentions of the candidate.

The bigger question is, as an interviewer what can you do about it?

Johari Window

The Johari Window model was developed by American Psychologists, Joseph Luft and Harry Ingham in the 1950s while researching group dynamics. How does the Johari Window help interviewers?

It increases their understanding not just about themselves but also of the others around them and therefore, enabling them to have a better and clear understanding of the relationships they have. Now the question is "How?" To answer this question, one must know what each of the four panes is.

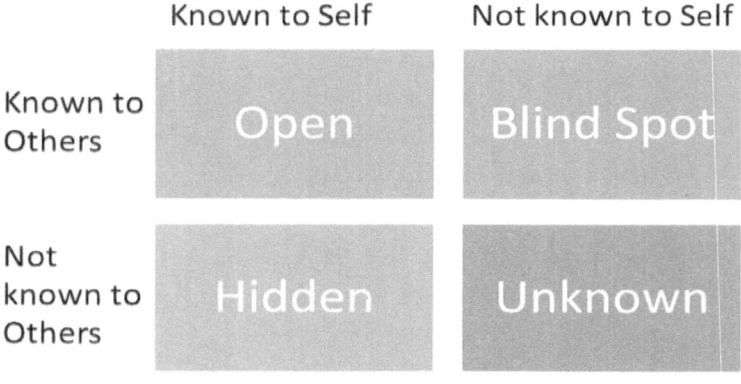

The Johari Window (Luft, 1969)

The first pane, called the **"Arena"** or the open window, holds information that I know about myself and the others around me are aware of. It is in this area where there is a free and open exchange of information and the communication is transparent.

The second pane, called the **"Blind Spot"** holds information that I do not know about myself but others around me are aware of (for example, clearing my throat before I say something, maintaining no eye contact while having a conversation or fidgeting during a presentation). These behaviours are observable but often can go unnoticed by the individual himself/herself.

The third phase, called the **"Facade" or "Hidden Area"** holds information that I know about myself but the others around me are not aware of. To keep certain things hidden from others takes a conscious effort from my side. This may include my personal information or anything that I am not comfortable sharing with people. This may arise from fear of being judged or looked down upon. Information in this area can also include one's thoughts, feelings and beliefs about a topic or situation.

The fourth pane, called the **"Unknown"** holds information that neither I nor the people around me are aware of. It may contain information from memories of early childhood, unresolved conflicts or latent potentialities. The boundaries of this pane change only when we grow up, start to understand and realize things about ourselves. This can be in the form of feedback sought and received.

Also, keep in mind that the sizes of the four panes are not equal and differ with every individual. The healthiest Johari Window is the one with Arena being the biggest pane. For example, a candidate who is an introvert will not talk unless and until probed. He/she will provide only monosyllable answers which make it difficult for you as an interviewer to gain information.

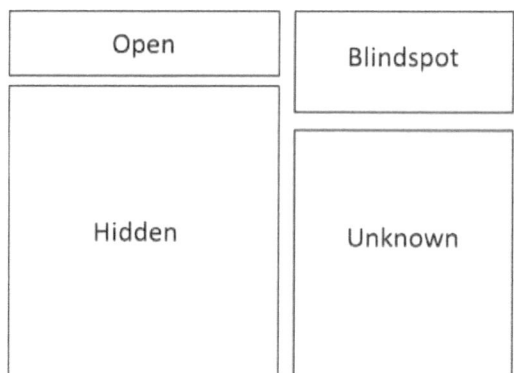

This is how the Window of an introverted candidate would look like. The hidden and the unknown area will be big, because of the lack of information provided.

With respect to unmasking candidates at interviews, Johari Window can be explained as follows:

Arena – this pane is open to both the interviewer and the candidate himself. It includes basic information like name, date of birth, place of residence, educational qualification, etc. The increase in this area will depend on the level of rapport the interviewer is able to build with the candidate. Therefore, we see how with an increase in trust and comfort, the boundaries of Arena will also expand.

Blind spot – These are observable behaviours that go unnoticed by the candidate and therefore his/her original behaviour that presents itself. This pane, hence, has information that will be noticed by the interviewer, if he/she is more observant. It can either be positive or negative behaviour.

Facade/Hidden – This pane contains information known only to the candidate. The interviewer will not be aware of this information without the candidate being willing to reveal it to him/her. The details here may include personal details about the family's background that he/she might not be comfortable sharing. The fear of being misjudged or misunderstood will withhold the candidate from being open and share information with the interviewer, which in some cases could be vital for evaluating the candidate. Information of this type will be disclosed only if a level of trust is established and the candidate is willing to widen the boundaries of this area.

Unknown – This is the pane of no information. Here both the interviewer and the candidate are unknown to the information. Hence it becomes the most difficult pane to reduce in size. This happens because of a lack of self-knowledge or belief. The only way to expand this unknown area is by understanding one's experiences along with constant feedback and discussions.

How Does it Help You Understand the Candidates Better?

The key to this lies in objectively debunking the existing mind-sets, die-hard habits and concrete-wall-like attitudes behind every behaviour and action displayed by an individual during the interview and mapping the same in line with the required competency and position in the job.

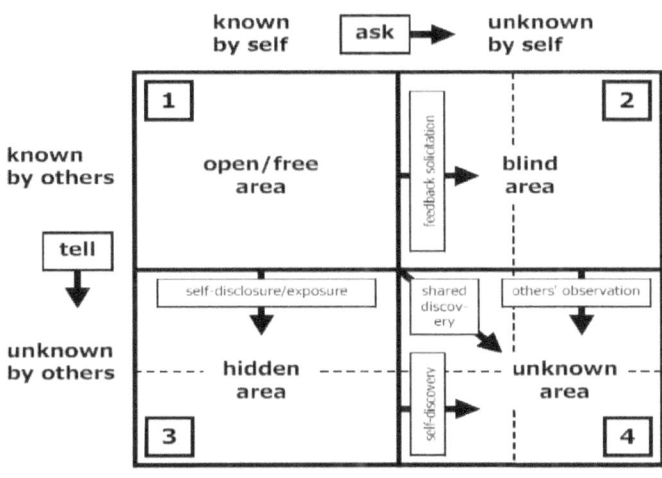

Johari Window model

In today's day and age, the Johari Window model becomes very relevant due to the modern emphasis on behaviour, attitude, empathy, cooperation, inter-group development and interpersonal development. Qualities such as these displayed in candidates we recruit or employ make a vital difference to the organizational growth and development.

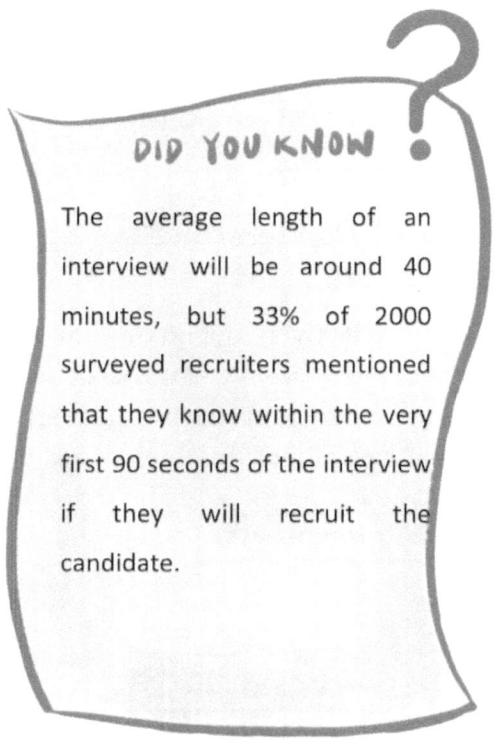

DID YOU KNOW

The average length of an interview will be around 40 minutes, but 33% of 2000 surveyed recruiters mentioned that they know within the very first 90 seconds of the interview if they will recruit the candidate.

Chapter 3

BAT—Behaviour, Attitude, Thinking

*"If you don't like something change it.
If you can't change it, change your attitude."*
- Maya Angelou

Research shows that individuals tend to form an immediate and automatic reaction of 'good' or 'bad' towards everything and anything they encounter in less than a second, even before they are aware of having formed an attitude.

Let us take the example of Rohan, who was invited by his friend Neha for an art exhibition featuring local artists. Despite being interested in art, Rohan finds this a waste of his time but agrees to go anyway.

As the day of the exhibition neared, Rohan still saw it as a complete waste of his time and had a ripple effect even on the day of the exhibition. His attitude began conjuring thoughts of boredom, tedium and his behaviour clearly indicated a lack of interest, overt indifference and a strong desire to be someplace else.

The above example shows how our Thinking, Attitude and Behaviour are interlinked and the three make us who we are. It is difficult to change our attitude and behaviour in order to adapt to new/existing situations. The reason being, attitude is inherited and developed over the years by our surroundings and behaviour is something that we pick up from these surroundings which is the result of a trapped environment we live in. As a result, it makes us difficult to change/modify our thinking as it is both directed and fuelled by our attitude which in turn influences our behaviour. Thus, we see a chain reaction taking place here.

How Does One's Attitude Impact Their Behaviour?

Attitude: It is a way of thinking or behaviour that is needed to fulfil responsibilities.

Aptitude: It is a natural ability that prepares a person to fulfil responsibilities.

Skill: It is an acquired ability or experience that is needed to fulfil one's responsibilities.

Knowledge: It is the information and understanding that is needed to fulfil responsibilities.

Behaviour: It is a trait that becomes observable.

Therefore, it is wise to focus our complete attention on the only rescuer for our growth and progress, which is our 'THINKING'.

The power to do so is within each person and with the right amount of focus, we can observe a great amount of change in one's attitude and behaviour.

Matching the Right Person to the Right Job

"Hire an attitude, not just experience and qualification." - Greg Savage

While hiring an individual, one must keep in mind their life experience, knowledge, skills, attitude and education. You may be thinking, why?

A candidate is not just the product of his/her college degree but a culmination of experiences that they've (he/she has) received from repeated interactions with people. Their (his/her) skills are not that was only taught but what they (he/she) acquired during their lifetime. Their (his/her) attitude is not what it used to be during the early ages of their life but has been moulded and shaped throughout the years and all of these help impact his/her habits and mind-set.

One must ask when and where do a candidate's knowledge, attitude, skill and education match the job description and how does it favour the individual? Well, this is where the interviewer comes into the picture.

In recent times selecting the right person for the right job is one of the most important tasks that must be performed diligently. With the number of applications filling up for any vacant position, the responsibility of understanding the candidate lies with the interviewer. Apart from the educational qualifications and skills, outlook and attitude of the candidate are also to be assessed. The rule of any interview is 80:20, i.e. the interviewer does 20 percent of the talking while leaving 80 percent to the candidate. The interviewer must be highly observant while the candidate gives information.

Here is stating an example- When a candidate applies for the post of a graphic designer, he will most probably use statements like, "I see myself as a very witty person" or "I associate myself with the colour yellow as I am a very happy person" during his/her interview. This clearly shows us that the person is a visual learner which is the ideal requirement for a graphic designer. Therefore, connecting the dots will help the interviewer arrive at the right conclusion.

The biggest challenge faced by most organizations around the world today is the knowledge of what would help them the most, knowing their strengths or their weaknesses. The best managers around the world say that focusing on each employee's strength and managing around his/her weaknesses are the best ways to approach the challenge.

Unfortunately, many organizations are rebuilt around the exact opposite answer i.e., maintain each employee's strength as it is and work towards fixing his/her weaknesses.

As discussed in the previous chapter, no child is encouraged to develop his/her strength; similarly, no employee is given the space to develop his/her strength but is taught to live in and abide by the principle of managing/mending one's weaknesses.

If an employee who was chosen for his strength is appreciated for the same, he will be encouraged towards polishing it. He will start loving what he does and will perform better as he is given an opportunity to polish the strength. This will lead to both personal and organizational growth.

Aligning KASH with Job Requirements

You can now learn the art of conducting interviews the right way with a holistic screening approach to understand the candidate's

KASH – Knowledge, Attitudes, Skills, and Habits

K – "The beginning of knowledge is the discovery of something we do not understand"

—Frank Herbert.

A – "If you don't like something change it. If you can't change it, change your attitude."

—Maya Angelou

S – "The skill to do comes of doing".

—Ralph Waldo Emerson

H – "Motivation is what gets you started; habit is what keeps you going".

—Jim Ryun

Another way of analysing candidates using the KASH format is by understanding if the job description and role expectation match. If it does, then one can be sure that the candidate's knowledge (primarily education) is the right requirement for the job. Looking into the performance outcome and the candidate's concept of future growth, it will be easy to understand the attitude of the person.

For example, if the candidate does not have a vision for five years from now or a dream he/she wants to achieve, then the individual is not looking for growth. His competency will help determine the skills that are his strengths. By matching the competency and skill set, one can determine if the candidate is a good fit for the role. His team profile also helps to understand the kind of role that was earlier handled and the field of experience. Keenly observing the answers the candidate gives will, to a large extent, help determine some of the habits the individual possesses. If, for example, the candidate has changed a few jobs with the same/similar role description and team profiling, it can give hints about the person's job-hopping habit.

Interview Humour

Not the Best Fit

I'm the placement person at a trade school; we train phlebotomists, among other positions. One of the students went on an interview, and when asked if she enjoyed doing blood draws said that she really didn't like needles.

Chapter 4

The Science and Secrets of Unmasking Candidates

Psychology

It is the scientific study of the human mind and its functions, especially those affecting behaviour in a given context.

Before diving into cutting-edge psychometric tools let us understand the term Psychometrics and its various facets. The word is derived from the Greek word, "psyche" meaning mind and "metric" meaning measurements. Therefore, it factually means, "measurement of the mind" and we see how it is concerned with techniques of psychological measurement, which includes the measurement of knowledge, abilities, attitudes and personality traits.

Psychometric Assessments rose to prominence throughout the 20th century and today it is described as the standardized assessments which look at human behaviour and describe it with scores or categories. With the increased access to these tools, it can be applied to assess and develop people from all spheres of life.

The biggest question is: How can these tools be used in an organizational setting?

The personality of a person is a unique set of attitudes, behaviour and thoughts that defines him/her. While no single definition of personality is accepted by psychologists, the most famous definition was given by Gordon Allport who stated, **"Personality is the dynamic organization**

within the individual of the psychophysical systems that determines his unique adjustments to the environment". The word 'personality' comes from the Greek word *'persona'* which means 'mask'.

Hence, these tools become really important for the organizations' HR while assessing the personality of a candidate they wish to hire. Current psychological articles suggest becoming more introspective in order to suit the vast complexity of modern people's development. However, one should keep aside the notion of "One size fits all" as people's personalities are far more complex.

Based on research inspired by the works of Carl Gustav Jung, the candidates belong to a combination of four personality types heavily influenced by natural heredity factors:

1. 'Feeler'—The Emotional Candidate
2. 'Intuitor'—The Idea Candidate
3. 'Thinker'—The Logical Candidate and
4. 'Sensor'—The Action Candidate

To identify **'Feeler Candidates'**, one can look out for behaviours like:

1. Concerned with reactions of others than objective reality
2. Enjoys dealing with Moods, Feelings and Emotions
3. Learning is verbal and by touch
4. Lives in the past
5. In tune with others' feelings
6. Good Team players
7. Sensitive
8. Sentimental
9. Warm and friendly; sometimes seemingly too much so
10. Doesn't seem to distinguish between business and personal conversations
11. Likes to gossip as they are in a world of emotions
12. Talks non-stop once they are comfortable

13. Feels rude if you interrupt in between
14. Demonstrate a personal approach

*Refer: **Holistic Approach to Personality, Psychometrics and You**[1]*

See Annexure: Fact Sheet for Psychometric Assessments

BEHAVIOURS OF FEELER CANDIDATES	
Ineffective	**Effective**
Impulsive	Spontaneous
Manipulative	Persuasive
Over-Personalizes	Empathetic
Sentimental	Grasps traditional values
Postponing	Probing
Guilt-ridden	Introspective
Stirs up conflict	Draws out feelings of others
Subjective	Loyal

Likely Blind-spots of 'Feeler Candidates':

1. Spend too much time talking about the past
2. Oversimplify
3. Do not rely too much on data
4. Do not push to bring objectives out in the open
5. Avoid bringing unpleasant facts to the surface
6. Use self-pity as a crutch
7. Forget to cite facts—tell too many anecdotes or stories
8. Bear grudges

To identify **'Intuitor Candidates'**, one can look out for behaviours like:

1. Future-oriented
2. Love to dream

---

1   *Chapter 8, page 26-71*

3. Form BIG Picture

4. Full of IDEAS

5. Integrate experience

6. WHY behind each What...!

7. Being told is not enough... Must discover from personal experience

8. Mostly in the world of imagination

9. Go off on tangents

10. Not mindful of others' time

11. Concentrate too much on the concept

12. Does not give importance to 'how'

13. Impersonal in one's approach

BEHAVIOURS OF INTUITOR CANDIDATES	
Ineffective	Effective
Unrealistic	Original
"Far-out"	Imaginative
Fantasy-bound	Creative
Scattered	Broad-gauged
Devious	Charismatic
Dogmatic	Intellectually tenacious
Impractical	Ideological

Likely Blind-spots of 'Intuitor Candidates':

1. Scattered in their comments

2. Jumping about too much

3. Raise too many issues

4. Be too lengthy

5. Come across as rigid

6. Appear to look-down on others

7. Be too abstract
8. Leave issues "dangling," unresolved
9. Concentrate too much on the concept; not enough on the "how"

To identify **'Thinker Candidates'**, one can look out for behaviours like:

1. Strong need to be correct
2. Gather facts rather than Ideas
3. Logical
4. Systematic
5. Organized
6. Structured, systematic approach to Learning
7. Enjoys collecting and processing information
8. Much attention to detail and precision
9. Business-like but lacks personal warmth
10. Tick off specifics – (a, b, c, or 1, 2, 3, 4)
11. Little voice interaction, persons of few words
12. Speak in an ordered, measured manner
13. Sometimes suggest ground-rules for conversation, for example, "Shall we begin with your agenda or mine?"

BEHAVIOURS OF THINKER CANDIDATES	
Ineffective	**Effective**
Verbose	Effective communicator
Indecisive	Deliberative
Over-cautious	Prudent
Over-analyzes	Weighs alternatives
Unemotional	Stabilizing
Non-dynamic	Objective
Controlled and controlling	Rational
Over-serious, Rigid	Analytical

Likely Blind-spots of 'Thinker Candidates':

1. Over explain
2. Be too noncommittal
3. Do not express feelings enough—lack affection
4. Appear too much to be driven by rules and regulations
5. Get involved in asking too many questions
6. Want to organize in too rigid a fashion
7. Give people more background than they really want
8. Assume that others are equally interested in technical subjects
9. Overly formal in the way they do things

To identify **'Sensor Candidates'**, one can look out for behaviours like:

1. Here-and-now.
2. Action-oriented.
3. Learn-by-doing.
4. Goal-driven.
5. Result-oriented.
6. Restless.
7. Drive away anxiety through 'action'.
8. Tapping feet/fingers while the mind races at 75 mph.
9. Gets to the point; expect others to do the same.
10. Command.
11. Interrupt.
12. Need to control the conversation.
13. Brief and fast.
14. Do not ask enough questions.

BEHAVIOURS OF SENSOR CANDIDATES	
Ineffective	Effective
Don't see long-range	Pragmatic
Status seeking	Assertive
Self-involved	Directional
Act first, then think	Result-oriented
Lack trust in others	Objective
Dominating	Competitive
Arrogant	Confident

Likely Blind-spots of 'Sensor Candidates':

1. Try to resolve things too quickly/talk too fast
2. Come on too strong, overwhelm others/command
3. Be so sure of oneself, they might sound arrogant
4. Insist that others agree with them
5. Cut corners to get what they want/scheme, connive even if unwarranted
6. Over-compete; translate non-competitive activities into win-lose situations
7. Do not take time to listen to objections of others/do not ask enough questions
8. Be proud to a fault
9. Use contacts with the opposite sex to feed their own ego

Based on the extensive research inspired from the works of Dr William Moulton Marston, one can easily observe four different dimensions of a Candidate's behaviour:

The candidate mirrors the various personality styles based on one's upbringing and environmental response since young, which are classified as (4C's):

Controlling (C1), Convincing (C2), Conforming (C3) and Consistent (C4).

No one style is better or worse than the others, and all four styles are present in each of us and them.

C1 is '**Controlling Candidate**'—the drive to overcome barriers, seek challenges, and achieve results.

C2 is '**Convincing candidate**'—the desire to win acceptance of others through one's popularity and ability to persuade.

C3 is '**Conforming Candidate**'—the desire to work within well-defined standards and controls to assure compliance.

C4 is '**Consistent Candidate**'—the desire to perform at a steady pace and maintain group harmony.

All the candidates display *these four dimensions of behaviour, though in* *different mixtures* *and* *to different degrees*

Characteristics of 'Controlling Candidates':

1. 'Controlling Candidates' have the drive to overcome barriers, seek challenges and achieve results.
2. They are typically anxious to get immediate results.
3. They accept challenge readily, make decisions quickly, and take charge of situations to get things done.
4. Strongly action-oriented, they question the *status quo* and look for new or better ways of achieving results.
5. They are happiest when tackling and overcoming a difficult problem or obstacle.
6. They prefer a broad area of operation and freedom from controls.
7. They dislike red tape and love to work with minimal supervision.
8. Such people are fuelled by the need to achieve by prestige and the challenge of their work.
9. They seek out opportunity for individual accomplishment.

10. They are most productive when given difficult assignments, personal accountability, direct answers, power and authority commensurate with the task.

11. When formal authority is lacking, they will assume it and bank on their power to get things done.

12. The 'Controlling Candidates' tend to be impatient with others and often perform alone rather than as team members.

Behavioural Indicators of 'Controlling Candidates':

1. Dislike inaction
2. Competitive
3. Low tolerance for feelings and attitudes
4. Work quickly and impressively alone
5. Quite impatient
6. Change-catalyst
7. Fear being taken advantage of

Behavioural Descriptors of 'Controlling Candidates':

Independent, self-reliant, assertive, vigorous, pioneering, tend to dominate, outspoken, strong-willed, decisive, persistent, argumentative and want direct answers.

Characteristics of 'Convincing Candidates':

1. 'Convincing Candidates' have a desire to win the acceptance of others through one's popularity and ability to persuade.

2. Typically anxious to make favourable impressions and share their infectious enthusiasm with others.

3. Welcome social situations and enjoy contacting people and making new friends.

4. Often have a colourful or vivacious personality, are entertaining and articulate, and manage to create an environment that draws others to them.

5. Work best in an environment that gives them freedom of expression and encourages democratic relationships.

6. Often active in group activities and are most productive when freed from details and controls.

7. Use their ability to verbalize ideas, influence people and persuade others.

8. Good at shaping the opinions of others, either as individuals or in groups where coaching and counselling skills are important.

Behavioural Indicators of 'Convincing Candidates':

1. Spontaneous in taking decisions and actions

2. Like involvement

3. Dislike being alone

4. Can exaggerate and generalize

5. Dream and get others to dream

6. Jump from one activity to another

7. Work quickly and excitingly with others

8. Seek esteem and belonging

Behavioural Descriptors of 'Convincing Candidates':

Disorganized, emotional, confident, like change, playful, fear loss of social approval, talkative, like recognition, create enthusiasm, like stimulating, desire to help, and motivated by appreciation or recognition.

Characteristics of 'Conforming Candidates':

1. 'Conforming Candidates' prefer to work within well-defined standards and controls to assure compliance.

2. Are excellent at following procedures and meeting the prescribed standards.

3. Focused more on detail and are sticklers for accuracy.

4. They are usually diplomatic with others and are analytical, deliberate thinkers.

5. There is great respect for authority, both of individuals and systems (policy, procedures, controls, standards).

6. They work best in an environment that is highly structured and well-defined.

7. Such persons require documentation of the job to be done—standard operating procedures, job descriptions, checklists, etc.

8. They prefer the status quo and ensure that quality controls and standards are met.

9. They often require personal attention, close supervision, reassurance that they are doing well (frequent performance appraisals), and strong membership in their workgroup.

10. They are best utilized on work that is exacting or precise in nature, requiring careful planning and close attention to detail.

Behavioural Indicators of 'Conforming Candidates':

1. Cautious while taking decisions/actions.
2. Ask questions with specific detail.
3. Want to be right; rely on data.
4. Work slowly and precisely.
5. Seek security, self-actualisation.
6. Possess Problem-solving skills.
7. Motivated by being on the "right way".
8. Fear criticism of self and their work.

Behavioural Descriptors of 'Conforming Candidates':

Well-disciplined, soft-spoken, devout, humble, obliging, rigid to changes, agreeable, orderly, perfectionist, sensitive, accurate and use critical thinking, not comfortable out of their comfort zones.

Characteristics of 'Consistent Candidates':

'Consistent Candidates' are usually good at calming others, listening and getting the facts, sticking with an assignment and being loyal to the organization.

In short, the Consistent Candidates support the status quo and provide a steadying influence on the workgroup. They demonstrate the desire to perform at a steady pace and maintain harmony. They are typically best at performing an established work pattern that requires patience and does not require travel or change of environment. They have typically developed specialized skills or technical competence and are able to concentrate on a given task or project for a long time.

Behavioural Indicators of 'Consistent Candidates':

1. Make decisions carefully.
2. Dislike interpersonal conflict.
3. Don't pay much attention to goal-setting.
4. Work slowly and cohesively with others.
5. Have counselling skills.
6. Motivated by the use of traditional procedure.

Behavioural Descriptors of 'Consistent Candidates':

Obedient, thorough, cautious, accommodating, satisfied, generous, loyal, enjoy recognition for their efforts, and look to bring everyone in a group to agreeable terms.

Long before we were born (even before the nine months, to be precise), the dice of 4C's were thrown and we received certain genes and chromosomes from our parents.

You probably recognize in one or both of your parents some of the same characteristics that we just used to describe the dimensions(s) that you were high in. Thus, heredity had a strong hand in shaping your behaviour.

But So Did The Environment. The way in which you were raised, the people who have influenced your life, the training and education you received, and the kinds of jobs and assignments you've had ... all these have also helped to shape your behaviour.

To ask which is more important—heredity or environment—is like asking whether the area of a rectangle is influenced more by its length or by its width.

In one sense, we are constantly growing—learning new things, meeting new people, handling new assignments. These exert an influence on us, and our "repertoire" of behaviour is enlarged accordingly. However, on the basic dimensions of our personality with which this exercise is concerned, most of our growth and development took place in the first place.

New Behaviours

Persons who are high on conforming and consistent who decide to become controlling and convincing are not likely to succeed unless the environment gets changed dramatically and their survival depends on the development of these new behaviours.

Since the work environment rarely changes dramatically and since our "personality clay" is fairly well-set, what is the value of knowing one's 4C characteristics and behaviours? Simply this: productivity, job satisfaction, and teamwork depend upon having the right faces in the right places. A team of quarterbacks is just as useless as a team of blockers. We need to work with others whose profiles supplement and complement our own. Both parties benefit, as does the work.

When selecting people for assignments on a team or task force, it is important that the nature of the work environment be analysed so that people can be picked who possess the characteristics that will be most at home in such an environment. The right match is essential to a "win-win" outcome, both for the individual and the organization.

Behavioural Pattern Analysis (BPA)—Behaviour Pattern Analysis Based on the Research of B.F.Skinner

It is easy to observe the different patterns of behaviour in the candidates. Every candidate is different, and they do exhibit such differences in the course of the selection process beginning with their resume, the telephone call or the face-to-face interview. Behaviours are behaviours; there's nothing right or wrong. But the differences in behaviour enable you to pick the right candidate for the right role.

These behaviours are nothing but conditioned or programmed based on one's environmental factors. Meaning, behaviour patterns are changeable from one situation to the other. However, due to the repetitive nature of home, school or work environments, the behaviours can get fixated. We can even refer to them as glue-like mind-sets or die-hard habits.

As an interviewer, when you wish to unmask the candidate, it is important to consider four major parameters like

1. Communication Styles
2. Interpersonal Relationships
3. Sense of Urgency and
4. Information Processing

Diplomatic Communicator	Strongly Diplomatic	Tend to be Diplomatic	Flexible Approach	Tend to be Outspoken	Strongly Outspoken	Outspoken Communicator
Introvert Relationships	Strongly Introvert	Tend to be Introvert	Flexible Approach	Tend to be Extrovert	Strong	Extrovert Relationships
High Sense of Urgency	Strongly High Urgency	Tend to be High	Flexible Approach	Tend to be Low	Strongly Low Urgency	Low Sense of Urgency
Innovative Approach in Processing Information	Strongly Innovative	Tend to be Innovative	Flexible Approach	Tend to be Systematic	Strongly Systematic	Systematic Approach in Processing Information

As you probe the candidate's suitability, in these four parameters you will notice strong behaviours or the candidate's tendency to tilt towards either of the two extremes. Healthy behaviour is the one that is in the middle path, demonstrating a flexibility to suit specific situations.

Communication Style of Candidates:

- **Behaviour of Diplomatic Candidates**—They are very careful in the way they express their views. This might help maintain healthy relations with one's colleagues and others. They influence people through a supportive and tactful approach. They are very calm and composed people, who prefer to negotiate than get into arguments. They are careful not to offend others while presenting their ideas and opinions, coming across as modest. They are good at collaborating and maintaining excellent relationships with people from different walks of life.

The strengths of the diplomatic candidates include:

✓ Being a good mediator and facilitator by keeping one's own issues in the background.

✓ Phrasing comments carefully so as not to offend others or push one's own agenda.

- **Behaviour of Outspoken Candidates**—They express their ideas with confidence and thus being influential. They tend to 'tell' rather than 'ask'. They take charge especially in situations that need control and clear directions and are perceived as being forceful and self-assured. They prefer to confront conflicts and openly debate differences. They are confident in presenting ideas that may result in overstating them at times. They state their position on issues candidly and frankly. They openly argue or debate their points of view or opinions. They come across as overconfident and tend to influence others with an assertive, outspoken approach.

The strengths of the 'Outspoken Candidates' include:

✓ Taking charge, especially in situations that need control and clear direction.

✓ Getting vague or hidden issues out in the open and restated in a frank, 'outspoken' way.

Behaviour of Candidate's Interpersonal Relations:

- **Behaviour of Introvert Candidates**—They prefer working alone and keeping emotions and feelings to themselves at the workplace. They would not be an active member in groups and gatherings. They interact very less with their friends, associates and colleagues. They enjoy spending time in solitary activities. Being a person who interacts and participates less in group activities, they would prefer solving their problems on their own. Seen as a trustworthy person for the organization, they maintain confidentiality by not giving in.

   They are most at ease interacting with others, one on one and tend to keep their emotions rather private and self-contained. They get energized when alone and away from activity. They prefer to think problems through by themselves, to clarify feelings. They use few gestures and facial expressions when they talk.

   The strengths of the 'Introvert Candidates' include:

   ✓ Being a good listener and feeling comfortable with letting others talk more than themselves.

   ✓ Holding information confidentially and not giving it away by expressing one's emotions.

- **Behaviour of Extrovert Candidates**—They are at ease when interacting with people and group. As an extrovert, the person shares emotions openly and freely with others. They keep in touch with their friends and well-wishers regularly as they feel charged up by connecting with people. They are most at ease interacting with people and groups and tend to share emotions openly and freely. They get energised by people-relationships and lots of activity. They prefer to talk problems and clarify feelings rather than holding it back. They use lots of facial expressions and gestures when they talk.

   The strengths of the 'Extrovert Candidates' include:

✓ Being good at establishing rapport, putting people at ease and making them feel important.

✓ Staying connected and up to date on personal issues that friends and stakeholders may be going through.

Sense-of-Urgency Behaviour:

- **Candidates with 'High Sense of Urgency'**—They consider a few important options before deciding and get things done by acting fast and making changes. They prefer short-term projects that require quick responses. A fast-paced style of work is usually observed in people with high sense of urgency as they do not enjoy procrastinating or extending deadlines. They react sharply when frustrated and angered. They make speedy decisions often. "Opportunity knocks but once". They prefer to act fast and make one's choices without postponing. They would be able to act effectively at the spur of the moment. Since they would value only required points, they would eliminate unnecessary options while at work or in solving problems.

  The strengths of the 'High-Sense-of-Urgency Candidates' include:

  ✓ Taking fast action when an opportunity arises that require an immediate decision.

  ✓ Getting clarity on what they believe are key priorities and eliminating options that seem to confuse the issue or delay action.

- **Candidates with 'Low Sense of Urgency'**—They consider many options and alternatives before deciding and get things done by "sticking with them" and persisting. They prefer long-term projects requiring calculated responses. They work with an even-paced, consistent style. They react slowly when frustrated and angered. Decisions are made cautiously—

"Timing is everything". Their style of working is smooth and slow-moving, which may frustrate the person's co-workers.

Their strengths include:

✓ Holding back on decisions until better opportunities and deals have time to surface.

✓ Patiently staying open to alternatives and possibilities that show promise and that others may have closed their minds to.

Information-Processing Behaviour:

- **Behaviour of Innovative Candidates**—They tend to postpone organizing and attending to details and use unconventional procedures to accomplish tasks. They like plans that are open and somewhat unpredictable and proceed on projects before reading all the directions. They take pride in doing things in different ways. They get frustrated by too many guidelines and rules. They may be capable of generating extremely novel ideas with respect to work. However, being very innovative, they may postpone organizing and attending to details while attending to any task. They could find innovative ways to improve systems and policies in the organization.

The strengths of the 'Innovative Candidates' include:

✓ Discovering innovative ways to search goals that may be outside of the traditional guidelines.

✓ An ability to overlook considerable disorganisation and get work done in situations that would bother most people.

- **Behaviour of Systematic Candidates**—They tend to organize details in a timely and thorough fashion and use established procedures to accomplish tasks. They like clearly set plans and somewhat predictable and proceed on projects only after reading all the direction. They take pride in doing things in proven ways. Adopting to a highly systematic approach, they tend to get frustrated by ambiguity and lack of specific guidelines to carry out any task.

The strengths of the 'Systematic Candidates' include:

✓ The ability to bring order and structure to unorganized situations.

✓ Seeing ways to improve systems and policies that help make workflow more even and smooth.

Behavioural Indicators of Candidate's Competencies—PPC 20

Evaluating and unmasking competencies is imperative for optimizing potential and unlock superior performance. Competencies provide a clear and *integrated set of dimensions against which performance* can be described and measured.

A well-designed competency framework can be used as the foundation of an organization's talent management strategy, providing the link between human resources and tangible business outcomes.

'Individual competence' is the behavioural characteristic of candidates that enables them to perform successfully in a job or a role. This includes the dimensions of skills, individual characteristics and what are termed as traits and motives. Competence is a dynamic interaction between components of job competency and levels of application.

Managing Change	Initiative, Risk Taking, Innovation, Flexibility/Adaptability
Planning and Organizing	Analytical Thinking, Decision Making, Planning, Quality Focus
Interpersonal Skills	Oral Communication, Sensitivity, Relationships, Teamwork

Continued...

Result Orientation	Achievement, Customer Focus, Business Awareness, Learning Orientation
Leadership	Authority/Presence, Motivating Others, Developing People, Resilience

The traditional achievement and intelligence scores may not be able to predict job success, wrote, David McClelland the famous Harvard Psychologist in the American Psychologist in 1973. One needs to profile the exact competency required to perform a given job effectively and measure them using a variety of tests. (PPC 20—People Performance Competency 20—along with FITS based on Carl G Jung and 4C's based on the research of Dr William Moulton Marston is a meaningful array of assessments to bring out the true strengths of the candidate.)

While unmasking candidates it is important to probe the candidate's past to understand one's behaviours in different situations and with different people. The competencies are directly linked to the candidate's behaviour. Here is a list of ten behaviours under each of the 20 generic competencies. As you listen to the candidate's explanation of one's behaviour in different work or life situations, you can get to see the true competencies through the past or current behaviours. One can easily make out whether these respective competencies are present in the candidate or not.

Competency mapping is the process of identification of the competency required to perform successfully a given job or role or a set of tasks at a given point of time. It consists of breaking a given role or job into its constituent tasks or activities and identifying the competencies needed to perform the same successfully in terms of observable behaviours.

Behaviours to look for in Candidates for INITIATIVE

1. They are prepared to do whatever it takes to bring about a change.
2. They are adventurous and like to take new steps.
3. They like doing what they say.

4. They often take the first step.
5. They are practical and have a hands-on style.
6. They like to take the lead in most situations.
7. They act independently when needed.
8. They are quick to take advantage of opportunities.
9. They take steps early to get towards results.
10. They make a start without further delay or postponement.

Behaviours to look for in Candidates for TAKING RISK

1. They question custom and tradition.
2. They are prepared to bend the rules.
3. They are willing to take risks.
4. They are willing to break with the past.
5. They question the way things are done.
6. They challenge rules and procedures.
7. They thrive on change.
8. They cut through red tape.
9. They are ready to take new directions if needed.
10. They often do and think differently.

Behaviours to look for in Candidates for INNOVATION

1. They make things happen.
2. They are very creative.
3. They originate change.
4. They think laterally and out of the box.
5. They like to tinker with and improve things.
6. They need the stimulation of change.
7. They generate fresh approaches.
8. They try out new ideas.
9. They can easily get bored with routine work.
10. Always look for a problem-solving, solution-finding approach.

Behaviours to look for in Candidates for FLEXIBILITY/ADAPTABILITY

1. They handle change with an open mind.
2. They give in a little when necessary.
3. They adapt quickly to new situations and are flexible.
4. They are prepared to go along with what others want to do.
5. They compromise to get an agreement.
6. They are ready to modify plans if necessary.
7. They will try to keep harmony and peace.
8. They can adjust to any situation and environment.
9. Look for ways to work out a mutually agreeable solution.
10. Make good mediators and negotiators.

Behaviours to look for in Candidates for ANALYTICAL THINKING

1. They zero in on the key issues.
2. They think things through.
3. They break problems down into smaller parts.
4. They analyse things before acting.
5. They make logical and rational decisions.
6. They display confidence in their own judgement.
7. They sieve through the information.
8. They evaluate and consider options carefully.
9. They will consider all angles before making decisions.
10. They get into details with a systematic approach.

Behaviours to look for in Candidates for DECISION MAKING

1. They make well-informed decisions.
2. They are confident about the decisions they make.
3. They are not hesitant to make decisions.
4. They are quick to act on their decisions.
5. They take responsibility for their decisions.

6. They are prepared to make difficult or unpopular decisions.
7. They deal with problems quickly.
8. They make sound decisions even under pressure.
9. Tend to decide based on available facts without delay.
10. Like to resolve issues and work on answers.

Behaviours to look for in Candidates for PLANNING

1. They work in a neat and organized way.
2. They never leave things to the last minute.
3. They prioritize their work activities.
4. They tackle tasks systematically.
5. They organize their time effectively.
6. They can draw up detailed plans.
7. They plan how deadlines are going to be met.
8. They are always ready and prepared.
9. They are sure of what they are doing as they have planned the work well.
10. They are well-prepared before they start any task.

Behaviours to look for in Candidates for QUALITY FOCUS

1. They never leave problems behind them.
2. They often finish jobs.
3. They have an eye for details and get the details correct.
4. They deliver on schedule.
5. They are systematic and methodical.
6. They often get involved in the details.
7. They set very high standards and expectations about the task at hand.
8. They can find the smallest mistakes/faults in tasks.
9. They can be counted on to get the job done accurately.
10. Strongly believe in precision.

Behaviours to look for in Candidates for ORAL COMMUNICATION

1. They are excellent orators.
2. They assert themselves in most situations.
3. They are good at selling ideas.
4. They are good with words and languages.
5. They can make effective presentations.
6. They are skilled at public speaking.
7. They will express themselves clearly and concisely.
8. They are good at convincing others.
9. They come across as very confident individuals.
10. They are not hesitant to talk to others.

Behaviours to look for in Candidates for SENSITIVITY

1. They consider the views of others.
2. They involve people in decisions.
3. They explain their decisions to other people.
4. They respond to people in a helpful manner.
5. They always consider other people's problems and concerns.
6. They make time to listen to people.
7. They often ask others for their viewpoints and opinions and genuinely consider it.
8. They are sensitive to people's needs and feelings.
9. They come across as very approachable individuals.
10. They come across as warm and caring individuals.

Behaviours to look for in Candidates for RELATIONSHIPS

1. They relate well to people.
2. They are people-oriented.
3. They get to know people quickly.
4. They enjoy being surrounded by people.
5. They are outgoing in nature.

6. They are lively and enthusiastic.
7. They have a wide range of contacts.
8. They have many friends.
9. They are good at networking with people.
10. They are the ones who will keep in touch with old friends and contacts.

Behaviours to look for in Candidates for TEAMWORK

1. They are easy to work with.
2. They are strong team players.
3. They work best in a team.
4. They enjoy being part of a team.
5. They are group-oriented.
6. They are helpful and supportive.
7. They cooperate with people.
8. They support each other.
9. They collaborate with people to achieve goals.
10. They strive to improve team effectiveness.

Behaviours to look for in Candidates for ACHIEVEMENT

1. They have the urge to win in all situations.
2. They take actions to achieve things.
3. They are ambitious and competitive.
4. They act as if work is the most important thing.
5. They focus on getting the job done.
6. They have the drive and determination to get to the top.
7. They can keep trying again and again till they achieve results and won't give up easily.
8. Want to **"make their mark"**.
9. They are highly task and result-oriented.
10. They are not satisfied with average performance and have a strong desire to succeed.

Behaviours to look for in Candidates for CUSTOMER FOCUS

1. They are patient with customers.
2. They are committed to quality.
3. They try to improve the service to the customer.
4. They respond quickly to customer complaints.
5. They strive for excellence in service delivery.
6. They understand the customer's needs.
7. They are courteous to customers.
8. They are good at building relations with the customer.
9. They like to delight the customer with the unexpected.
10. They make every effort to retain their customers.

Behaviours to look for in Candidates for BUSINESS AWARENESS

1. They focus on performance.
2. They use resources carefully.
3. They set tough business targets.
4. They keep up with business news.
5. They watch costs closely.
6. They manage money effectively.
7. They think about how to get more for less.
8. They keep abreast of the competition.
9. They have good knowledge of their profession and awareness of their competitors.
10. They are well-informed of all aspects of their business or industry.

Behaviours to look for in Candidates for LEARNING ORIENTATION

1. They address their weaknesses.
2. They seek ways to test themselves.
3. They ask for feedback and take the feedback positively.
4. They enjoy learning new ways of doing things.

5. They learn from their mistakes.
6. They know their own strengths and weaknesses.
7. They have specific learning goals.
8. They take charge of their own learning and development.
9. They are looking for opportunities to increase their knowledge.
10. They are always eager to learn and increase their skill sets.

Behaviours to look for in Candidates for AUTHORITY/PRESENCE

1. They pitch in and lead by example.
2. They have an aura of self-confidence around them.
3. They try to influence others through their charismatic presence.
4. They have presence and authority.
5. They are dynamic and vibrant.
6. They inspire confidence.
7. They enjoy being in charge.
8. They like to be in control of situations.
9. They are energetic and enthusiastic.
10. They have a strong need to get things done.

Behaviours to look for in Candidates for MOTIVATING OTHERS

1. They empower team members to help them grow.
2. They delegate tasks effectively.
3. They are good listeners and understand people's problem effectively.
4. They encourage their team members to grow and develop.
5. They use persuasion and expertise to motivate people.
6. They tend to trust others a lot to do the right thing thus they don't bother to focus on the trivial matters.
7. They inspire other people of their own capabilities.
8. Strongly believe in team members' talents.

9. Ready to help others to achieve their objectives.
10. Always stay positive in their outlook.

Behaviours to look for in Candidates for DEVELOPING PEOPLE

1. They go out of their way to help people develop.
2. They like teaching new skills to people.
3. They create a challenging climate to work in.
4. They try to act as a role model for others to follow.
5. They give opportunities to others to make them self-aware of their potentials.
6. They are very effective coaches.
7. They help people learn from their mistakes and empower them.
8. They are attentive towards the growth of others and thus will give regular feedback from time to time.
9. They like to nurture the potential of people.
10. They get people to perform to their fullest with support.

Behaviours to look for in Candidates for RESILIENCE

1. They are relaxed.
2. They are tough enough to handle any problematic situations.
3. Criticism is handled very positively by them.
4. They deal with setbacks effectively with a lot of patience.
5. Coping with stress is not a hurdle for them.
6. They are able to deal with difficult situations calmly.
7. They display self-control irrespective of the adversity of the situation.
8. They face situations head-on if need be.
9. They love challenges.
10. They are self-confident.

Leader's Effective Aptitude Profile

Recruitment takes place at all levels. However, one must be careful while hiring for a leadership post. This role would entail using the candidate's power to influence the thoughts and actions of people. It is therefore imperative to unmask the type of leadership skill each candidate embodies to choose the best out of the pool.

The four types of leadership according to LEAP are:

1. Organizer—Systems Driven
2. Coach—People-Person
3. Entrepreneur—Visionary
4. Specialist—Technical Expert

Characteristics of a Systems-Driven Candidate—Organizer

1. Leads by defining goals and organizing systems and resources for achieving them.
2. Places high value on conformity, order, control, paperwork, systems and accountability.
3. Driven by the desire for fail-safe systems procedure and stability.
4. Creates conditions for low risk and predictability.
5. Strongly influenced by past ways of functioning, "We've never done anything like that", etc.
6. Prefers smart work over hard work.

Characteristics of a People-Person—Coach

1. Leads by coaching, motivating and rewarding others to perform.
2. Places high value on loyalty, teamwork, self-discipline, commitment and cooperation.
3. Driven by a desire for motivated employee and teamwork.
4. Creates a condition for job satisfaction for employees.

5. Works keeping the present in mind, "Here's how we're going to do it" and "How can we best achieve our goals?"

6. Prefers getting done things through others.

Characteristics of a Visionary—Entrepreneur

1. Leads by providing a vision of how things might be in the future.

2. Places a high value on self-realization, inspiration, striving and change.

3. Driven by the desire for ideas, change, innovation and excitement.

4. Creates condition for high risk, flux and uncertainty.

5. Future-oriented and influenced by imperfect past, "What if we were to..." or "I've got an idea as to how we might..."

6. Prefers getting the right things done over getting things done right.

Characteristics of a Technical Expert—Specialist

1. Leads by example and personal experience in the chosen field of expertise.

2. Places high value on personal ability and individual excellence.

3. Driven by the desire for freedom to apply one's talent without hassle from others.

4. Creates conditions for job satisfaction for self-control of one's destiny.

5. Works in the present, "There's work to be done...let us stop talking and get it done." "How can we ever get all this work done?"

6. Prefers doing everything personally if you want it done perfectly.

Organizer as a Leader:

- They are the product of past conditioning
- They crave for order and the security of the status quo
- They sometimes view change as a threat, a source of potential problems and a disruption of their orderly system.

Coach as a Leader:

- Coaches fill a leadership role that is sometimes "boss" and sometimes "coach" while getting work through others.
- They crave teamwork—cooperation, consensus, and commitment.
- In filling their role as coach, they rely on goal-setting, training, counselling, delegating, disciplining and rewarding.

Entrepreneur as a Leader:

- Entrepreneurs see things not as they are but as they might be
- Everyday conditions challenge and spark this person to make them better... to see innovation, to experiment, to be a catalyst for change
- Entrepreneurs live in the future, a world of overabundant opportunities
- The entrepreneur's world is the conflict between boundless opportunities and people who don't share the vision and won't climb overboard

Specialist as a Leader:

- Specialists are their **own master.**
- They work best **alone** because they are happiest when applying their talents to the work at hand.
- They **work steadily** and **dependably**, one thing at a time, and have a need to control the work at hand.
- To the Specialist, **thinking** and **dreaming** are **unproductive.**

- The **"how-to-do-it"** right now is more important than planning for a new tomorrow or generating more efficient methods for today.

Therefore, selecting people for technical skills or knowledge alone does not guarantee success. Use the latest cutting-edge tools in Behavioural Sciences to get a thorough understanding of the attitudes, thinking styles, core competencies and personality patterns before you make the costly decision to hire.

How do psychometric assessments help in determining the same?

Let us begin with a few basic questions:

➢ What does an organization need in order to be successful?
  - Is it a brilliant idea that solves a big problem?
  - Or the disruption that it brings to the monopoly in the market?
  - The resources to sustain and grow?
  - Adapting to market conditions?
  - Or having the right talent across levels?

Let us look at some facts below:

1. In a study conducted by Employee Benefits News, it was concluded that the average cost of losing an employee is 33% of their annual salary

2. In the context of employee retention:
  - 34% of employees are more likely to quit within the next year if they don't feel valued at work. (Tiny Pulse)
  - Employees are more likely to stay longer at a company if it invested in their careers, a whopping 93% of them. (Gallup)

What we can gather from the above statistics is the importance of talent to run and sustain an organization. This is not to say that other factors that were brought out don't play an important role. We cannot, however, ignore that a talent's impact on an organization can either make it or break it. And hence, the root of creating a successful talent pool begins with choosing the right candidate.

Apart from educational qualifications and subject mastery, organizations currently have begun to understand that a "right person for the right role" is more than just the above-mentioned factors. What we additionally need is a candidate:

a. whose strengths match the required role basics
b. whose work style and personality complement the team
c. whose work style and personality complement the boss

To enhance human optimization, save valuable resources and reduce attrition, one needs to tackle the root-cause—the ATTITUDE through INTER(NAL)VIEW.

Psychometric tools help in being objective and capture various attitudinal dimensions like

➤ *Competency areas*
➤ *Personality styles*
➤ *Communication patterns*
➤ *Motivational levels*
➤ *Interests*
➤ *Preferences and a score of other important aspects*

Attitudinal Assessments

Assessment is an art. It needs a skilful blend of theory with hours of practice.

The benefits for the same include:

1. Job Profiling
2. Hire for Attitude—Train for Skills
3. Recruitment Solutions
4. Competency Mapping

5. Succession Planning
6. Training Need Analysis
7. Team Building
8. Performance Management
9. Performance Appraisal
10. Employee Empowerment
11. 360-Degree feedback

Let us examine a few cases.

'Moonbies' is a start-up organization, with a vision to launch a wide range of economically sustainable products for a greener world. Within this broad vision, the organization has several functions to achieve this shared goal, segregated as individual departments. The candidates required for each of these departments must be suitable and qualified for the function's requirements.

It requires five main functions to stabilize and maintain efficiency:

a. Business Development
b. Finance
c. Quality Control
d. Supply Chain Management
e. Engineering

Let us focus on the position of Business Developer—Apart from technical requirements, the company requires candidates who possess

- Relevant Experience
- A positive attitude towards tackling situations
- Strong negotiation skills
- Passionate about sustainable development
- Ability to work under pressure in a matrix organization
- Strong leadership skills (In managing and guiding one's team to achieve goals and facilitate the growth of everyone)

Apart from the mentioned requirements, the key to selecting individuals is to match them with the underlying competencies and their behaviour, which the interviewer must make note of.

In the context of **Business Development**, it can be explained further as a checklist:

- Creative and analytical ability—for problem-solving.
- Quick to establish rapport and build relationships—for getting new clients.
- Convincing Abilities—It is important for the candidate to possess negotiation and persuasion skills to manage external and internal stakeholders. The person in the position of Head of the Department will be expected to contribute to managerial discussions.
- Working under pressure and ability to manage ambiguity— Since the company is a start-up, it will be in a high state of flux and it needs people who can push through and not buckle down under pressure.

Let us take the example of two candidates Jeevan and Mathew. Both were asked to take psychometric assessments that measured their personality style based on their natural traits and environmental factors, their communication styles and behavioural patterns along with their current competencies. Based on the results, let us probe in-depth into their personalities.

Mr. Jeevan:

Looking at his **strengths**, Jeevan comes across as a

- Systematic, idea-driven individual who can value variety, challenges and emotions/feelings giving importance to accomplishment and people involved.
- Future-oriented, he tends to view things from a big-picture-perspective.

- He is likely to take his roles and responsibilities seriously and make well-thought-out decisions in policy, planning and financial matters.

- He can gauge the customers' requirements and deliver in accordance with the market demands. He has the ability to use this knowledge to anticipate future customers' needs.

- He has the potential to convey his ideas with clarity and shape people's opinions through his convincing skills which help in establishing and maintaining customer relationships.

- He has the potential to take charge and support the team to deal with challenging situations guiding them with inspiration and a positive appraisal.

- He can motivate his team members by empowering and delegating appropriate tasks to reach their potential.

- His ability to connect with people supports him in establishing a strong team to enhance business growth, thus coming across as a coach.

On the other hand, the challenges he could come across are:

- He takes time to decide as he gives importance to gathering facts/multiple perspectives and gaining others' approval.

- Remaining focused and composed in difficult and unfamiliar situations, he may take time to bounce back from failures or disappointments. This might affect his performance during such times.

- He may also need to work on setting accurate and realistic targets for the team members along with collaborating with people who can support him dealing with problems while taking a decision.

Now, the above summary can be compared to the checklist we have of the role expectations with results of the candidate to make a recommendation.

	YES	NO
Creative and analytical ability	✓	
Quick to establish rapport and build relationships	✓	
Ability to convince	✓	
Working under pressure and ability to manage ambiguity		✕
Manage team by inspiring and empowering them	✓	

Mr. Mathew

Strengths:

1. Organized and creative thinker: able to generate ideas and validate them at the same time.
2. Good at solving problems with his analytical ability when required.
3. Able to **plan** and **prioritize** his tasks in achieving tangible results.
4. He advocates continuous improvement and would be willing to go out of his comfort zone to enhance **knowledge** and **skillsets** in his field.
5. His interpersonal skills will allow him to build his **network** and act as an interface/support with peers/customers/dealers with ease.
6. Systematic in his approach, he can structure his own activities and those of others, coordinating the use of resources to maximize market potential.
7. He has the potential to communicate with internal teams and can negotiate effectively with clients and gain their buy-in while handling business deals.

Challenges:

- Being **task-oriented** and not innately attuned to pick up on **emotional subtleties** among people, he may at times overlook the needs and viewpoints of others.

- Tends to rely on his past experiences in **ambiguous situations**. Thus, he may take time to explore lucrative opportunities to expand the business in **untrodden areas**.

Now, the above summary can be compared to the checklist we have of the role expectations with the results of the candidate to make a recommendation.

	YES	NO
Creative and analytical ability	✓	
Quick to establish rapport and build relationships	✓	
Ability to convince	✓	
Ability to manage ambiguity		✗
Working under pressure	✓	
Manage team by inspiring and empowering them	✗	

If we compare the above two candidates, we see that the fundamental requirements of the function are satisfied, which can be gauged via the job description, interview and validated through psychometric assessments as well as to introduce objectivity. However, what the current recruiter lacks is 'situation-fitness'. In the example of Mr. Jeevan and Mr. Mathew, we see that Mr. Jeevan has a challenge in coping with stressful situations as well as situations with ambiguity. This is because, as an individual reliant on clarity and direction (either from his role or from his senior authority), he may not readily accept situations that lack structure and a clear set of guidelines. In the context of 'Moonbies', given that it is a start-up, and with functions that are still emerging, there are likely to be various situations where there is often a lack of clarity/structure. In such situations, Mr. Jeevan, although a candidate with various strengths, may not be suitable as the organization requires a candidate who can take control of situations, actively work on obstacles and deal effectively with adverse situations.

Mr. Mathew, on the other hand, can work under pressure but can find it challenging to manage during ambiguous situations. He may also not spend time to inspire and motivate his team and empower them of their potential. Lack of motivation in the team can lead to discontent and eventually, attrition.

If a decision has to be made between Mr. Jeevan and Mr. Mathew, based on role-fitness, we would consider Mr. Jeevan, given the added advantage that his leadership skills provide him. However, should the decision be made based on both role and situation-fitness, neither of them would be suitable. However, Mr. Jeevan would be a better candidate, with considerable training and coaching to help him manage his challenge areas of working under pressure in ambiguous situations.

In the case of **Finance,** the following can be taken as the criteria for employment.

- Preparation of budgets, forecasts and cash flows.
- Work as a trusted Adviser to the management and partner with them to increase the revenue and profitability.
- Strong Business Acumen for new Business deals by calculating strategic pricings and securing profitability.
- Budget Management—Planning/Resource management.
- Attention to Details.
- Structured/Organized.
- Weigh the pros and cons—deliberative, work based on facts.
- Managing team.

Like in the above case, let us take the profile of two candidates Walsh and Watson. Both were asked to take psychometric assessments that measure their personality style. Based on the results, let us probe in-depth into their personalities.

Mr. Walsh

Strengths:

- Inherently **inclined towards logic**, he prefers **working with facts** and is likely to collect information about a situation before arriving at a decision.

- **Weighing his options** for their pros and cons, his tendency to critically think through situations would help him in monitoring and analysis of the investments made.

- **Organized and systematic** in his approach, he is likely to delve into minor details with a focus on accuracy. This would enable him to maintain precision to meet the standards of quality required.

- **Methodical** in his approach, he would prefer to plan out his actions in detail, keeping into consideration priorities and resources. This, coupled with his detail-orientation, would help him maintain the timeline as well as the quality of work. This may help him manage cash flow, financial control, reporting, tax, audits and such.

- **Extroverted** by nature, he may find it easy to **build rapport and maintain relationships**, enabling him to build a network of contacts. Likely to articulate with clarity, he would be able to communicate effectively to share information. Thus, he would be an efficient point of contact for stakeholders.

Challenges:

- As a leader, when approached with an issue, he may not try to understand it from the perspective of the people to gauge what posed as the challenge. Further, working with the information provided, he **may not probe for further information**. Thus, while the problem is addressed at the surface level, it may not be resolved from the root, resulting in recurrence.

- While taking major decisions, he is open to the views and opinions of others and may bend over backwards to incorporate them. While this makes others feel valued, his emphasis on collaboration may result in him finding it challenging to work independently if/when required.

- His tendency to plan things in a detailed manner is likely to help him cope with adverse situations as he is likely to have back-up plans and contingency managing alternatives. However, the confidence he gains due to his all-encompassed planning may appear as a laid-back attitude to others, making them feel unsettled.

Now, the above summary can be compared to the checklist we have of the role expectations with the results of the candidate to make a recommendation.

	YES	NO
Preparation of budgets, forecasts and cash flows	✓	
Manage relationships with stakeholders	✓	
Strong business acumen for strategic pricing	✓	
Attention to Details	✓	
Establish systems / structure	✓	
Weigh pros and cons – deliberative, work based on facts	✓	
Working under pressure and ability to manage ambiguity	✓	
Manage team by inspiring them and empowering them based on their strength	✓	

Mr. Watson

Strengths:

- Being an idea-driven, analytical and action-oriented individual, he would validate his ideas to form an objective outlook on situations. His innate ability to be logical enables him to support his decisions with facts and figures.

- He can also identify problems and has the potential to break the problem down into simpler ones that enables him to troubleshoot challenges on time. He may use appropriate planning techniques based on priorities to meet the requirements of the assignment.

- Being an idea-driven, analytical and an action-oriented individual, he would validate his ideas to form an objective outlook on situations. With an ability to conceptualize the big picture while ensuring the details are not missed, he would be able to align his ideas with the requirement of the overall objective.

- Using his knowledge and expertise, he handles customers well and understands their needs. Keeping a futuristic outlook, he may think ahead and plan for the growth of the organization.

- His trust in his team's potential would help him motivate his team members by empowering and delegating appropriate tasks to reach their potential.

- Establishing rapport, he can connect with people and develop a large network of relationships. He keeps his interactions friendly and cordial and people do not hesitate to come to him for solutions.

Weaknesses:

- He is flexible in his sense of urgency, and thus he may accord his own priority for the completion of work and needs a little push for execution and completion of projects. He is a low risk-taker and is likely to be cautious in his decisions on various aspects of the business; the decision making, at times, could be delayed.

- Though good at articulating himself and with a genuine desire to help, he may not listen fully to his team members not understanding their point of view. Relying on team members' potential may let him assume that people will do what is expected of them within the given time. This may lead to disappointment when the expectations are not met within the stipulated time.

- Though he comes across as friendly, he may not pick up on emotional subtleties in other people and may be perceived as less empathetic in his communication while dealing with his team members or customers.

Now, the above summary can be compared to the checklist we have of the role expectations with the results of the candidate to make a recommendation.

	YES	NO
Preparation of budgets, forecasts and cash flows	✓	
Manage relationships with stakeholders	✓	
Strong business acumen for strategic pricing		✗
Attention to Details	✓	
Establish systems / structure	✓	
Weigh pros and cons – deliberative, work based on facts	✓	
Working under pressure and ability to manage ambiguity	✓	
Manage team by inspiring them and empowering them based on their strength	✓	

In the above example, a comparison between Mr. Walsh and Mr. Watson's profile clearly indicates the better fit for the role. Psychometric assessments can help identify the role fit in this manner. However, this is only an exercise to identify a better fit, and not label any candidate as incompetent.

The indicators used as references, focus more on behavioural competencies and a few skills required, and are not fully representative of all the factors to be taken into consideration to make a decision on hiring. For a strategic decision to be made on hiring, the recruiter must consider various other factors such as the description of the job, the resume of the candidate that highlights his/her experience as well as the performance of the candidate during the interview process apart from the behavioural competencies.

The above samples of indicators have been chosen in the specification to a start-up. Just as we have narrowed down the crucial competencies based on the culture of a start-up, the indicators can be drawn similarly for established organizations, and the rest of the process can be followed in a similar manner.

One has to keep in mind that the representation of cultural aspects is not to label start-ups/established organizations—this has been done to narrow down specific aspects that could be a necessary pattern for a start-up owing to the nature—thus, ambiguity, ability to work under high-pressure situations and ability to deal with a multiplicity of roles are a basic requirement. Similarly, for established organizations, it is most likely that they are highly structured and hence that becomes a requirement. The best approach, hence, is to understand each client's organization and culture, going beyond the JD. This is the opportunity to value-add and choose a candidate that is a good fit.

Let us now take a look at team profiling. Once a candidate has cleared all stages after he/she has been placed, we must try and understand how they fit within the team.

Let us say we have a team as below:

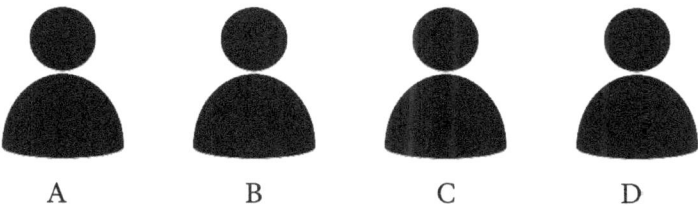

A B C D

Let us say that A, B, C and D belong to the Business Development team for which Jeevan (the candidate evaluated previously for the BD position) is hired to lead. For the profiling of the team, Jeevan's strengths and challenges would be interpreted alongside the strengths and challenges of each of A, B, C and D—based on the results from psychometric assessments.

This would help the management understand the interplay of each one's personalities/competencies/behaviour patterns to predict common areas of interest and anticipate areas of conflict.

Apart from individual analysis for recruitment, results from the psychometric assessments can be applied to a group as well—for Organization Development. This can be done to assess a team of different functions, as well as the management team at different levels. The benefit of doing so can help us understand where the team stands now and evaluate the gap to where they are required to be. In situations of evaluation, it is best to use assessments that involve multiple aspects and hence a battery is recommended.

Let us take an example with a single assessment that focuses on personality—to understand how group interpretations can work. Taking an average of all the scores of the team members results in a unified score that can be interpreted. The preferred way forward to analyse group profiles is through a SWOT analysis, as it helps the team understand where they stand as well as what the consequences of the same are—both positive and negative.

For sample and illustration purposes, let us consider the scores below as an example for the personality test.

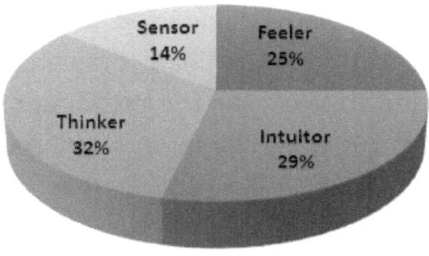

Sensor
Driven by action, Achievement-oriented, Pushes for immediate results, Focused on the here and now, Direct & to the point.

Thinker
Logical & Analytical, Organized & Systematic, Strong need to be correct, Driven by facts and figures, Keen eye for details.

Feeler
Driven by Emotions, Sensitive, People Oriented, Dwells in the past, Team player, Concerned with reactions of others.

Intuitor
Driven by ideas, Futuristic thoughts, Focused on big picture, Quest to know why behind each what, Needs variety & change, Must discover from personal experience.

Summing up, the orientation of 61% of the group is inclined towards a Thinker-Intuitor personality style which is attributed with characteristics of generating creative ideas that have a logical approach.

A lower percentage (39%) of Feelers and Sensors within the group indicates that emotions and orientation of action are relatively lower, respectively.

STRENGTHS	OPPORTUNITIES
• Focused on rational and objective evaluations • Gather facts before making decisions • Futuristic outlook, thus able to understand the consequences of actions • Generate creative ideas backed with a • logical and analytical insight • Take a holistic approach while attending to details in a systematic manner	• Creative problem-solving • Delivery of service/product with precision and quality • Design novel initiatives leading to new business opportunities • Anticipating problems • Objective decisions with a planned approach
CHALLENGES	THREATS
• A sense of immediacy is overlooked due to prolonged planning • Past mistakes might not be considered, thus repetition may cause • wastage of resources • Overlooking others' viewpoints in order to communicate one's own ideas • Reworking on the same project to accommodate new ideas, leading to stagnation	• Over-emphasis on tasks rather than people might lead to job dissatisfaction and attrition • Very less probability of implementation due to a tendency to focus on systems and precision, thus slow growth as a team • Over-cautiousness might lead to confusion and indecision

Thus, the group is likely to be involved with creating and deliberating over alternatives and options, rather than putting the ideas into action. Further, the priority is likely to be on tasks, while emotions of the people tend to be overlooked, which could lead to issues with collaboration.

Based on the above results, we can arrive at the following conclusions about the group:

To summarize, we have explored the below possibilities with psychometric assessments for recruitment and development:

- For Start-Ups and Established Organizations
- Selection of Candidate
- Team Profiling
- Organization Profiling

Psychometric assessments can be explored under various domains for development, further from recruitment as a value-added consulting for organizations.

References:

1. https://www.benefitnews.com/news/avoidable-turnover-costing-employers-big?brief=00000152-14a7-d1cc-a5fa-7cffccf00000andutm_content=socialflowandutm_campaign=ebnmagazineandutm_source=twitterandutm_medium=social
2. https://www.tinypulse.com/blog/13-surprising-statistics-about-employee-retention
3. https://learning.linkedin.com/resources/workplace-learning-report-2018

When you put a photo on a resume the chances of getting discarded are up to 88%.

Curse of the Cell phone

I was interviewing a candidate for a sales position. She was dressed professionally and had a year-and-a-half of experience. The interview was going very well for about 20 minutes when her cell phone started ringing. Instead of shutting it off, she answered it ad began talking to her boyfriend for almost a minute. I was astonished and told her that her interview was over. She didn't know why I cancelled the interview. All the better!

What do you think? Was it the right way for the interviewer to have done?

Unmasking Attitudes

"Who looks outside, dreams; who looks inside, awakes."

– Carl Jung

70% of the interviews today are competency-based!

What does this mean?

A competency-based interview is aimed to test the candidate's specific skills and attitudes. It provides candidates with an opportunity to talk openly and freely, without any inhibitions of the answer being wrong. These questions allow the candidate to talk about their experiences and how they dealt with situations in the past.

"We want to hear about candidates' previous experiences and understand how they would handle different situations in the future; so it is important to have thought about some examples ahead of the interview," says Helen Tucker, director of Human Resources of P&G Northern Europe.

While it has numerous advantages for the candidates, it is equally beneficial for the interviewers as well.

It **removes the risk of personal bias** and makes the hiring process fairer as well as helps interviewers **gain a clear understanding** of the individual's attitude and skills. Whereas in traditional interviews, the questions were centred on educational qualification, previously held posts/designations and the years of experience.

This method of competency-based interview will draw out the information necessary to establish whether a candidate will be likely to fulfil the needs of the job.

Let us consider a scenario where Akash, the HR Manager interviews Sumit for the role of Asst. Marketing Consultant. He could ask the following questions for each required feature:

- **Teamwork**—When was the last time you worked as a team to complete a difficult task?
- **Responsibility**—Have you ever taken responsibility for a difficult task at work or in your personal life?
- **Problem-Solving—How did you solve the above situation and what was the result of the same?**
- **Decision Making**—Did you have to make a difficult decision within a team that most people were against?
- **Communication**—How did you communicate and convince the decision to your team?

All the world's a stage,
And all the men and women merely players;
They have their exits and their entrances;
And one man in his time plays many parts,
His acts being seven ages.

-William Shakespeare (As You Like It)

It is basic human nature for people to mask their original self from the world to put a favourable impression of themselves. What they are in person may not be the same behind closed doors. As written by Shakespeare, the world is a stage and people are great actors. They act the way you would like to see and say to you what you'd like to hear. This holds, especially during interviews. That is why you need to rely on measurable tools from the world of Behavioural Sciences to get an Inter(nal)view.

Therefore, today's challenging recruitment procedures must pave way for psychometric assessments to assess the skills, intelligence and personality of a candidate. As per sources, it has helped in the hiring process of both budding companies and already established conglomerates.

Unmasking Attitude is a Process

In any interview, one critical part is asking questions about past behaviour. This may be in the form of questions about the person's past experiences or giving him/her a situation-based question and ask them what they would have done. The process of unmasking attitude is based on the principle that one's past performance predicts their future performance in a similar situation. The reason for this is that our attitudes are formed due to our past behaviours, habits and experiences. Therefore, they are more likely to exhibit the same if faced with a similar situation, again.

For example, if a kid was taught to help people, it is likely that this behaviour will be visible in the future as well. This may be portrayed as a character of a good team player who is very helpful.

INTER(NAL)VIEW focuses on examples of past behaviours that can be used to predict future actions, masked attitudes and/or needs. It is a systematic process that is structured and goal-oriented.

Let us consider the example of Sam, an HR consultant had an interesting story to share when asked about a past situation where he had to take control of something that was going wrong in the company. He said, "I was part of the sales and marketing team in my previous job. The company was doing well in terms of the business. However, I received several complaints from the women staff that they never received their due in terms of promotions, election of board members, etc. Even though it didn't affect me personally, I understood that they needed support from me as well as the others in office. So, I decided to step in and help them. I asked them to write a letter to the MD stating their concerns and to get it signed by all those who supported them in office. Upon receiving such a complaint, the MD took immediate actions and made sure to include female representatives in the board and consider them for promotions".

This indicates that Sam not only cares for his employees but also takes initiative to resolve conflicts that may not fall in the purview of his authority and reflects his ownership characteristics.

Process of Inter(nal)view

1. Start by Preparing

In most situations, the interviewee is more prepared than the interviewer. It could be because of the large number of applications that come in for one post that needs the eyes of the interviewer. This might be an additional workload but are these excuses relevant enough to come to an interview unprepared?

One must keep in mind that, as much as the candidate needs the job, that much you would need the right candidate. Hence, it is of utmost importance that you review the candidate's resume or application and review the interview-plan developed for the position to which the candidate is seeking employment.

Let us look at the following case studies:

a. Mr. Jose (a member of the interview panel): "Hey Stephen, our company has a few biases which make it harder for us to hire the right people. Now, what are we going to do with the two job-hopping candidates? Have you gone through their resume? Their professional career is loosely carved."

Mr. Stephen (another member of the interview panel): (Sighs) Well, I haven't yet. I was occupied with some projects. Let us just get done with it quickly. (Laughs)"

Mr. Jose: "But, at least have a quick glance at the details of both the candidates. The first one, 30 years old, has experienced six different jobs! Absurdly versatile! The second one is 38 years old; he has explored fewer companies, but his professional record isn't holistic."

Amidst project deadlines, deficient employee strength, unmanageable business operations, and unproductively prolonged interview sessions, job-hopping attitude of candidates was the cherry on the top of a cake. But Mr. Jose, a promising HR professional, anyhow wanted to figure out ways to deal with these candidates.

(Finally, interview session began.)

Mr. Stephen: "I welcome you to our company. I have gone through your resume featuring all professional and personal details; let me take a leap. I am a little anxious to consider you for this position as you keep changing jobs every year. Convince me to hire you." (A gesture of keen observation follows.)

Much to the surprise of the interview panel, the candidate uttered a few words to define his strengths, qualities, virtues, to name a few. Mr. Jose, sitting on the other chair, was overwhelmed with the short-sighted question posed by his counterpart. The sessions involving both the candidates witnessed such restricted questions leaving the entire process insignificant.

This is a classic example of the interviewer coming to the interview unprepared.

b. On the other hand, Rohit waits in the room patiently for his interviewer to arrive. He didn't want to create a bad impression by arriving late and hence came 10 minutes early. Soon he was greeted by the HR Manager Gaurav Sahni. After taking their respective seats, they began the interview.

A well-prepared interviewer reflects not only a strong personality but also a strong work ethic and excellent work environment.

2. Arrive at Requisite Competency

The groundwork to conduct an INTER(nal)VIEW is to find out what "competency" is required to accomplish the job successfully. By making a list of competencies required for the job, it becomes easier to select the right person for the right job.

For example, ABC Co. listed down their most desired competencies. For further clarity, they broke down each competency into sub-competencies. By doing this, it becomes easier for the interviewer to regulate the interview process as he now clearly knows what he is looking for in the candidate.

1. **Entrepreneurship**
   - future orientation
   - ownership

2. **Performance abilities**
   - decision making
   - planning, organizing and execution
   - passion and commitment

3. **Interpersonal Dynamics**
   - communication
   - cooperation and collaboration

4. **Leadership Attributes**
   - empowerment and delegation
   - natural leader

The next step is to tick off those competencies (required for the job) that are visible in the candidate. This is most efficient through face-to-face interactions.

You may be wondering why!

3. The Critical Link

Through face-to-face interactions, one gathers not only information in the form of answers the candidate gives, but also information in the form of observable behaviour as portrayed by the candidate during the interview.

As described in the section on Johari Window, most often the candidates are not aware of the behaviours they show and therefore this becomes the best possible clue/information an interviewer can gather about the candidate. Why? Because he is not masking it.

Therefore, selection based on Behaviour and Competency is valid, reliable, and legally defensible. Focusing on behaviours helps reduce the impact of common interviewer errors. For example, the resume of a candidate might have said that he/she works well under stress and pressure. This might be the competency the company must be searching for also. However, how can one be sure of everything written on the resume? Keen observation along with role-plays can be used to gain clarity and insight into the candidates' working style.

4. Studying the CV

Curriculum Vitae means 'the course of one's life'. The CV is the most important document the candidate provides. Studying the CV is an integral part of the selection process and it serves several important purposes.

The CV contains information such as educational qualifications, strengths, number of years of experience and positions held, personal details, etc. Therefore, studying the CV beforehand can save you a lot of time. It also will help you, to a large extent, to identify if the candidate will fit in the role. Previous job roles can give you this information. This helps to weed out unsuitable candidates.

DID YOU KNOW??

The first CV was sent to the Duke of Milan in 1482 by Leonardo Da Vinci.
Instead of listing down all his abilities, he put himself in the duke's shoes and figured out what he could offer to make his position better.

Linking Educational background to behaviour: Education plays a major role in shaping an individual's Behaviour, Attitude and Thinking. Most often the subject chosen by students in school/college is because of the interest they take in it. The next obvious question is, how does this interest arise?

The reasons can be many. Parents, peers, siblings, etc. can act as an influence. While the persons mentioned above do play a role, education too acts as a catalyst to help determine the subject of interest. The more an individual learns and understands a subject, the more he/she is immersed in it. This brings about a change in the thinking, attitude and therefore the behaviour of the individual.

Let us take the example of Sreya. She's been a student of psychology for five years and as a result, she sees the mind as the most powerful. She practices positive thinking and gives more importance to empathy over sympathy while trying to understand the situation from the other person's perspective. Thereby, she is seen as highly empathetic and understanding to people around her.

This shows how education impacts the behaviour of an individual as well as gives the interviewer vital information about the candidate. Therefore, for the hiring process, it is imperative to select a person whose educational qualification matches their job requirements. This can be done by looking at how consciously the educational path was chosen. This will help the interviewer understand if the candidate has a long-term plan.

While looking at the Goal-Orientation competency, give higher preference to the candidate whose education was consciously chosen to fit into a long-term career plan, that was realistic at the time and which has been successfully executed.

Let us take the example of a civil service aspirant, Gauthami. Throughout school, she had an affinity to subjects like history, political science, etc. She was always sure of doing something in the public service and all her activities throughout school and college reflected this decision of hers. She went on to do her B.A. in Political Science, where she got more insight into the functioning of government and the role of civil service. She then goes ahead and joins a coaching centre to help her clear the exam. During this process, she also pursues her M.A in Sociology as it was closely related to her career option.

Here we see how each of her educational qualifications is in tandem with the desired path of her career.

To go one step further, the candidate's Alma Mater also plays a significant role in shaping the individual.

Similarly, a student who wanted to pursue medicine and become a cardiac surgeon chose to take physics, chemistry and biology as his main subjects. He focused on getting into the top medical institutes in the country. He consciously chose to do internships in the same department (cardiology) and went on to do his masters and specialize in the same field.

5. Identifying Career Progress

One can determine a lot about the candidate's fitness for the job by looking at his/her past job experience. Creating a trajectory of their past performance will help draw the future path of the candidate. This trajectory may include the job role, responsibilities as well as the previous salary of the candidate. To get a better, bigger and a more specific picture, one can add the educational background as well.

For example, Pranav has recently applied for the role of an Assistant Regional Manager, Sales. He has worked for two-and-a-half years in his previous organization and is looking for a better opportunity to grow. This is the first time he is looking for a change in job. If we were to create a trajectory for Pranav, it would look like this:

Education—MBA

Previously held jobs—1. Sales Manager

Role responsibilities—Negotiate business proposals and sales contracts, maintain market awareness and manage his sales territories

Salary earned—Rs. xxxxx

Other areas of focus should include:

- Look for candidates who always climb the vertical ladder and not the horizontal.
- Look for candidates who aim one step higher each time.
- Look for candidates who are ready to work hard to achieve the higher step.

Following are the indicators to look out for, if:

- The candidate has progressed rapidly
- The candidate has had several jobs without making significant progress
- The candidate has spent more than five years in the same job

These indicators do not always imply there is a problem, but it is worth targeting in the interview. Don't be too quick to judge the candidate at this stage.

6. Open and Structured Interview

The interview room was big and well-lit and had a huge table in the middle. Two well-dressed men sat facing each other. One was in his late twenties while the other seemed a little older, maybe in his forties. While one was well-prepared for the interview, the other one seemed confused as to how to start the interview.

By now, you might have guessed that it was the interviewer who was the confused one.

Sometimes, even after studying the resume of the candidate repeatedly, the interviewer may still seem confused about what to ask or the direction in which the interview progresses. Therefore, it is a prerequisite to always structure the interview so that there is a clear idea about the entire process and gives the interviewer the desired result. Greeting the candidate by name, settling into the interview can be the first step. This becomes the interviewer's initial opportunity to establish a rapport with the candidate in a one-to-one setting. In addition to setting the tone, the interviewer should also accomplish several specific tasks.

One should:

- Explain the purpose of the interview and the areas that will be discussed.
- Assure the candidate that, to be fair and consistent, all applicants are asked questions about the same competency areas.
- Reinforce that there are no "right" or "wrong" answers.
- Explain that you'll be taking notes throughout the interview process, so you'll have accurate information on the candidate and no information will be missed or ignored.
- Inform the candidate that he or she will have the opportunity to ask you questions about the organization and job role at the end of the interview.

Skills that will help you – There are several skills which can help make you a more effective and more confident interviewer, an interviewer who ensures the candidates feel comfortable and easy to speak to, an interviewer who can easily churn the information out of candidates, a recruiter who is most valuable to the organization, an interviewer who will hire the right person for the right job.

Keeping just a few key points in mind can help you achieve all the goals mentioned above.

1. **Establishing Rapport**
   - Provide the candidate with a calm atmosphere
   - Express and project feelings similar to that portrayed by the candidate
   - Maintain candidate's self-esteem
   - Show empathy
   - Provide encouragement and support

2. **Effective listening**
   - Maintain eye contact
   - Be open to all possibilities
   - Paraphrase and summarize
   - Take note of non-verbal cues
   - Give importance to information gathering
   - Ask questions to gain further additional information
3. **Efficient Questioning**
   - Ask for specific examples that are job-related
   - Probe for further information and details
4. **Exhaustive and accurate note-taking**
   - Capture complete behavioural examples
   - Record verbal and non-verbal actions
5. **Effectuallypace the interview**
   - Establish boundaries and limits
   - Refocus
   - Transition
   - Strengthen and reinforce brief answers
6. **Ending the interview on a positive note**
   - Respond to questions the candidate has
   - Clarify next steps
   - Thank the candidate

Example 1:

The interview room was filled with silence.

"If there was one thing in your past that you could go and change, what would that be?" asked an interviewer. At first instance, this question may seem irrelevant to the current scenario as it has nothing to do with the description of the job. To an interviewer trying to beat the clock with respect to completing the interview process, this question would come across as redundant.

Ahead of this question, the panel of interviewers struggled to encourage the candidate to reveal his dream job, strengths and weaknesses, the decisions in his life which he regretted and his current expectations from professional life. The interview session was going through a rough patch of annoyance on the part of interviewers and uneasiness on the part of the candidate. The interviewers were not able to comprehend the introvert candidate. So, what was stopping them from asking the right kind of question?

This is how it started...

Interviewer: Hello, please take your seat and introduce yourself.

Candidate: Hi, my name is Vishal Diwan and I'm from Bhopal. I've worked as a Senior Engineer and am looking for better opportunities. That is why I have applied to this position.

Interviewer: So, what do you think are your greatest strengths and weaknesses?

Candidate: Well, ummm, I'm not very sure how to put it. However, people think I'm a good listener and that I can remember things quickly. But I can't relate to too many people at a time. Language could sometimes be a problem which hinders effective communication. I am making a conscious effort to rectify this. **It is like writing with your left hand.**

Interviewer: It is great that you're taking a step forward.

This undoubtedly appealed to the candidate who seemed more relaxed than before and revealed more about himself which was the motive of the interview—**Identifying the Right Candidate**. Comfort filled the room. Finally, the interview trick dug out valuable contribution from the candidate too.

Gone are the days when interview sessions used to witness conventional and predictable questions stressing only on candidate's work profile, his monetary expectations and discussing the joining date. This kind of straightforward interaction leaves no room for analysing a candidate's mind-set. Whereas, stimulating questions provide the candidate with the opportunity to share his/her best skill sets, experience and aspirations. By doing so, the interviewer too gets to see how closely the candidate is aligned with the responsibilities of the position.

Now, it is the sole responsibility of the entire panel of interviewers to discover open-ended questions to allow the candidate to speak freely and without any inhibitions, thereby enabling the interviewers to do justice to the procedure of the interview right from the initial phase itself. Truly, in an era coupled with tricky distractions and ambiguity which make it difficult for almost all candidates to take the right decision and contribute in the growth of a company, deciphering such recruitment tricks that involve a series of mind-revealing questions is the need of the hour, isn't it?

Let us consider another example.

As the elevator door dings, Rohit enters a well-lit room with walls painted white. His eyes soon fell on the grey colour contrast wall adorning the company logo and vision. The office was on the 17th floor of Sunshine Towers in Dadar and provided a beautiful view of the city. Rohit takes a deep breath soaking in all that he can as his nerves have slowly started taking over him. He soon heard his name and nervously, yet with a smile entered the room to find two men across the table. He greets them both and proceeds to take his seat.

The two men introduce themselves as Mr. Sen from the HR department and Mr. Radhakrishnan, the Senior Publishing Editor.

Mr. Sen: So, Rohit, tell us how you are today? How did you reach our office?

Rohit: I took public transport, Sir, as I don't drive myself to interview.

Mr. Sen: Oh, why so?

** Rohit didn't have an answer. He was reluctant to reveal that he was too nervous to drive himself to an interview safely as his mind would be preoccupied with what could go wrong during the interview.

Mr. Sen (sensing his discomfort): That is completely understandable. I too prefer to take public transport to avoid Mumbai traffic. Anyway, let us continue. Why don't you share your background with us?

Rohit (In a tensed mumble): Sir, I'm Rohit Sharma. I was born and brought up in Mumbai and am currently residing in Malad. I just completed my M.A in Mass Communication from Mumbai University. This is my first interview and I think that your organization will help me start an excellent career.

Mr. Radhakrishnan: That is interesting. Your university has a good reputation for providing competitive and successful people like Mukesh Ambani, B.R Ambedkar, Vidya Balan, etc.

Mr. Sen: I agree. It does have strong alumni.

Mr. Radhakrishnan: Well, Rohit, let me brief you about what we do. As you know, we're a publishing house that comes out with books, magazines and journals to name a few. We've been around for a decade and a half. Our company not only revolves around delivering the best content solutions that exceed the expectations of our clients but also provides excellent career opportunities to our team. Since you've applied for the position of Junior Publishing Editor, your main responsibility will be to go through the entire content before publishing it; you shall be provided with insightful training for the same. So, do you think you'll be able to take up such a huge responsibility?

Rohit: (nervously) Yes, Sir.

Mr. Sen: Rohit, do you want to have some water? Or let us have a cup of coffee.

Mr. Radhakrishnan: Why not?

Mr. Sen: What are your interests, Rohit?

Rohit: (feeling comfortable). Sir, I like to read fiction novels and write journals. I mostly explore travel blogs online. Also, I enjoy watching movies with friends, especially the classics.

Mr. Radhakrishnan: Interesting! So, your interest is in par with the position we are looking for.

DID YOU KNOW ?

- The average time spent by recruitment managers for analysing a resume is: 5 to 7 seconds.

- Unprofessional email addresses are the reason for rejection of 76% of resumes.

Chapter 56

Unmasking Behaviours through Inter(nal)view

Ask Structured Questions for Identifying Behaviours

Behaviour is the result of attitudes, habits and thinking. It is the observable part of an individual. Behaviour in the environment can be caught through questioning. These questions are structured in such a manner to understand and catch those behaviours exhibited by a candidate in an event/situation. These questions may not necessarily have any relation to the information provided in the resume.

Structuring Questions

What is the outcome of asking questions? What do I wish to gain out of it? What am I looking for? These are some of the questions that have to be kept in mind while structuring questions to identify candidates' behaviours. Forming questions based on the competency list of your organization will help provide you with answers that can help understand the candidate's behaviour, attitude and thinking.

Three Steps to Gathering Behavioural Evidence

An interviewer will need information that will help you predict how a candidate will perform in the job.

When you are conducting an interview,

1. You must look for factual evidence that provides a full picture of how a candidate approaches certain situations.

2. You must ask the candidate to tell you about specific situations, what he/she said or did in each of those situations and what the result of the action was.

3. Then use the behavioural evidence that you gather in the interview to evaluate the candidate in each of the critical dimensions.

Let us look at an interview, where Meera, the department head interviews Jay, her first candidate for the day.

Meera: Good morning, Jay. How are you doing today?

Jay: Good morning, Ma'am. I'm fine, thank you.

Meera: I have taken the liberty of going through your CV. But please tell me more about yourself.

Jay: I hold a master's degree in Economics and have worked in a few organizations before. The experience I've gained from them is what makes me qualified to take up a challenging position in your organization.

Meera: It's good to see your confidence. But why do you want to leave your current employer?

Jay: I'm a stickler for company policies and that's why changing policies and an unfair approach adhered to by existing organization didn't bode well with me. If an employee has invested his time and energy in nurturing and implementing an idea, his efforts deserved to be recognized rather than taking it for granted.

Meera: Could you give me an example from your life that can shed light on this issue?

Jay: Yes, I and my team of three were working on a project. Although I had the most experience, I wasn't made the team lead. Also, the team didn't have much idea on what to do and since it was a team project, my effort wasn't appreciated.

Meera: Did you consider guiding your other team members?

Jay: Well, technically it wasn't my responsibility. Hence, I didn't do so. Also, I'm not very comfortable with sharing my work with others.

Meera: Don't you think that at the end of the day, you would be burdened with more work than called for? Why do you find it difficult to share your work?

Jay: I perform better when I do it alone and don't mind taking up work. However, I will not tolerate the fact that I am not appreciated for the work I do.

Meera: From the experience you shared, I understand that you're a one-man army. Also, you prefer not taking up responsibility until called for. Am I right?

Jay: I don't shy away. But I felt it was not right to interfere because the responsibility was not mine.

Meera: Ok. Has there been any instance where you took the initiative to lead your team in your previous organization?

Jay: (thinking) Hmm.... No, Nothing I can think of.

Meera: Alright. It was great talking to you. I will let you know if you get selected!

If we had to break this interview down to understand it better, the interviewer Meera made sure she got all the information she needed. Let us assume that the competency she was looking for in a candidate was teamwork. She probed Jay accordingly and made him elaborate a situation and dug deep to understand the candidate's perspective.

Recognizing Factual Evidence and Seeking Behavioural Responses:

Factual evidence is nothing, but information supported by facts is more real. But how do you determine that the information provided is indeed true? One can use the following tips to keep the interview real and based on facts rather than being pretentious.

- A person stating facts is most likely to speak in the first person and use 'I' rather than 'We'.

- Similarly, he/she is more likely to speak in the past tense—'I did' rather than 'I would'.

- A real interview would entail the candidate describing a specific situation rather than generalizing what to would do or what would typically happen. Words like usually, typically, sometimes, always, generally, etc. should raise red flags.

- An interviewer should look for action words rather than evaluative words. E.g. If a candidate states that he usually has a great rapport with his customer, it is the interviewer's responsibility to probe further and ask how he/she managed to maintain the rapport.

Tell, Sell and Close Interview

This is the part where the interviewer does the talking. After probing into the candidate's BAT—Behaviour, Attitude, Thinking and asking the right questions using the KASH analysis, one is ready for the next three crucial steps.

DID YOU KNOW

- It is worthy to note that only 35% of the candidates are eligible for the jobs they apply to.
- Applicant Tracking Software, the automation software for reading resumes, can eliminate over 75% of the applicants.

- Tell the Candidate about the job—the roles and responsibility along with the candidate's opportunity for growth within the organization. The mission and vision of the organization need to be explicitly mentioned to the candidates.

- Sell to the candidate as to why joining your organization is the right thing to do. Help them understand what the organization does and how it is better from the rest.

- Close the interview on a positive note and clear doubts of the candidate if any.

Chapter 6

Guide to Behavioural Questioning

"Behaviour is the mirror in which everyone shows their image."

– Johann Wolfgang von Goethe

The requisite for a great business is its human resource. Therefore, it is imperative to hire people who not only have the right skill, but also the potential to do great things in their role, in a team and in the company.

Screening candidates during an interview can be a tedious task, especially with them masking their original personalities to please the interviewers. Most often interviewers analyse the candidates by their traits and unique perspectives. Yet a 30-minute conversation can be insufficient to fully understand the person.

This is where behavioural questioning paves a way to revealing a person's potential with respect to their ability to adapt, grow, collaborate, prioritize, lead, etc.

Therefore, the primary task of an interviewer is to obtain complete examples that provide a full picture of how the candidate would react when faced with certain challenging situations. Hence, it is important that interviewers **look for CAPE.**

Just like Clark Kent becomes Superman with his cape and Bruce Banner becomes Batman, every candidate masks his original personality during interviews. The CAPE gathers complete behavioural information from the candidate about the **Condition** or **Activity**, the **Performance** of the candidate, and the **Effect** of that action for each situation described.

Looking for CAPE will help the interviewers identify the behavioural responses of each candidate, thus allowing them to select the right one.

Look for CAPE

- Condition/Activity—the circumstance, situation or task
- Perform—how the candidate responded
- Effect—the impact (effective or ineffective)

Condition or Activity

The Condition/Activity is the background or context the candidate has already been in. It explains the reason as to why the candidate behaved as he or she did.

Condition or Activity are created by occurrences such as:

- Changes in the job responsibilities or work processes of the candidate
- Demands made by a manager or customer
- Challenges in meeting a deadline or in getting along with a co-worker

Examples:

"My team had been working without a break for weeks on the company profit presentation which the board would review next week. But due to change in schedule, the presentation got pushed to tomorrow."

Perform for Effects

Effects are the outcome of the candidate's performance. They tell us what changes or difference the person's actions made and whether the actions were effective and appropriate.

Example:

"Although the deadline was pushed, everyone in the team worked together to make it happen. The plan was to see what motivated each of the team members and push him or her to do her part accordingly. They gave their best; no one ever got burned out. Everyone felt appreciated, and no one seemed to mind making some extra money. And we really celebrated when our office topped all the sales records for the quarter."

CAPE is a method to identify the candidate's past behaviour in each situation. It goes one step further by identifying the effect of his/her actions had on the team/organization. This will help the recruiters to choose the right fit for the job as well as the team and the organization.

Types of Behavioural Questions

While gathering behavioural evidence of any candidate, keep in mind the three types of questions during the interview process:

CHIEF QUESTION

- Requests a detailed example of job-related behaviour
- Usually asks what the candidate has done (past tense)
- Is open-ended
- Does not signal a "correct" answer

ENQUIRE

- Requests further information
- Is open-ended
- Usually begins with—Who -/What/Where/How/When

**You should probe when the information given:

- Is not specific
- Does not provide a complete answer
- Is not given in first singular person
- Needs further clarification
- Does not match the behaviours listed for that competency

RECAP

- Redirects or checks for understanding

Example: Maddy is briefing his junior on how to conduct his first interview.

***Maddy: Remember the three most important questions you must not miss out. Start the interview with the chief questions that must be open-ended. Questions like what the candidate did in the past, the job description, how the experience was like, etc. Next, you should enquire more to gather more information. These questions usually are the 5W and 1H questions. Make sure you keep them open-ended. If you are not clear with the information, do not hesitate to ask again. Finally, give a recap of the information you have collected about the candidate. This will aid in correcting if there was any misunderstanding or mistake and give the candidate the confidence that he/she was listened to throughout the process.

Taxonomy of Educational Objectives — Benjamin Bloom (1956)

Benjamin Bloom (February 21, 1913– September 13, 1999)

He was an American educational psychologist who made contributions to the classification of educational objectives and to the theory of mastery learning. He is particularly noted for leading educational psychologists to develop the comprehensive system of describing and assessing educational outcomes in the mid-1950s.[1] He has influenced the practices and philosophies of educators around the world from the latter part of the 20th century.

https://en.wikipedia.org/wiki/Benjamin_Bloom

Bloom explained the Taxonomy of Educational Objectives. This was created for the purpose of classification of different learning objectives the teachers set for students. This will help in selecting appropriate classroom assessment techniques.

Organizations today have adapted the Taxonomy to evaluate candidates and their performance. To understand the higher-order thinking skills in candidates, Bloom identified six levels of cognitive complexity in the design of questions.

- Knowledge Rote skills—ability to recall facts, terms, procedures, classification systems
- Comprehension—The ability to translate, paraphrase, interpret, or extrapolate material
- Application—The capacity to transfer knowledge from one setting to another
- Analysis—The ability to discover and differentiate the component parts of a larger whole
- Synthesis—The ability to weave component parts into a coherent whole

- Evaluation—The ability to judge the value or use of information using a set of standards

While using this during the recruitment process, the interviewer can unmask the candidate by dwelling deep into each of the six aspects.

- **How well can the candidate recall facts and figures?**

E.g. What were the highest and lowest targets you achieved in your previous organization? Did your team follow any procedure to achieve these targets? If so, could you elaborate on the same?

- **Is the candidate well-adept at translating information to his team or others?**

E.g. What according to you is SEO (Search Engine Optimization)?

- **How well does the candidate transfer information up, down and across?**

E.g. Elaborate on a situation where you had to pass information to your team members as suggested by the Senior Management team

- **How well does the candidate analyse information about the organization?**

E.g. With respect to your previous organization, can you tell us how the organization ran as a whole with the interdependent roles of each of the departments?

- **How well can the candidate incorporate two different ideas/ concepts/department?**

E.g. If you had to corroborate Maslow's Hierarchy of Needs and the Needs Theory, how would you do it?

- **The candidate's ability to make judgements and decisions**

E.g. If you had to increase your sales without compromising on the workers' hours of work per day, how would you be able to achieve your target for the year?

Did you

Kn⊙w ?

The average length of an interview will be around 40 minutes, but 33% of 2000 surveyed recruiters mentioned that they know within the very first 90 seconds of the interview if they will recruit the candidate.

Chapter 7

Be Mindful

There are a few things that an interviewer needs to keep in mind during the interview process. One needs to:

Effective Listening

You might be listening to the candidate. But are you really listening effectively? Does the candidate know that he has your full attention? How do you know you are listening effectively? If not, how can you listen effectively?

- Make sure you're well-read and well-prepared
- Watch out for interruptions and take action/steps to prevent them
- Give the candidate your full attention
- Maintain eye contact
- Have an open mind
- Don't interrupt

There are candidates who give you a lot of information, more than what is required and then there are candidates who hardly speak. There are candidates who lie and there are those who are honest with sharing information. There are candidates with minimal hand and body gestures and there are candidates who are very expressive with body movements. In any of these cases, effective listening will help you get the information you need—said or unsaid. Effective listening also gauges you to ask accurate questions. This will effectively direct the interview the right way.

An HR executive recalls an interview she was a part of two years ago. She says, "I once conducted a group discussion session for four candidates who applied for the role of Content Designer. In my one-decade long career where I have conducted hundreds of group discussions, this will always be my favourite. It is because all the four candidates were completely different from one another. While it was challenging, it was also interesting to see how different each of them was. While I had to constantly cut off the talkative extrovert, the introvert had to be probed each time for a response. The other gave unrealistic answers when asked to share personal experiences making it very difficult to believe. And the last person would give information that had to be kept confidential and was extremely open and honest with his feelings, thoughts and ideas.

Through effective listening, I was able to pick out information from each of the candidates. The extrovert was a planner, the introvert was an idea person, the one who had unrealistic answers had trouble with self-esteem and the person who was honest turned out to be extremely sensitive."

Documenting Responses

Note-taking is a skill interviewers use throughout the interviewing process to help in remembering what the candidate said. As you take notes during the interview, you should try to capture as much content of the actual responses the candidate gives. It is worth the effort to hone one's note-taking skills. It helps to remember critical information about the candidate.

Taking thorough and accurate notes in an interview yields many benefits:

- Taking notes keeps you focused on the important job of collecting CAPE. When documenting information, you can see which parts of the CAPE are missing and determine the follow-up questions that will fill in the gaps.

- Good notes ensure that your impressions of the candidates and their answers don't blur together in your mind.
- Later in the process, when you share information on candidates with other individuals, your notes will provide them with an insight into the discussion.

Note-taking comes to the rescue while conducting interviews for a large group of people and during group discussions. Knowing the importance of note-taking is not enough. As an interviewer one should also know what notes to take.

Gathering unwanted information and writing down everything the candidate says will not allow you to concentrate on the important information. Therefore, it is essential that we know what notes to take. Put into paper that information that you think is required and closely related to the profile of the job the candidate is being interviewed for.

Sometimes the notes will also include the interviewer's observations about the candidate. For example, an introvert candidate's fidgeting provides many unsaid pieces of evidence. The fact that he is nervous and is not a talker will aid in making judgements. These are crucial information that can be discussed with the team members, to reach a conclusion.

Evaluate the Candidate

We have gone through several ways in this book to understand candidates based on their personality, interests, behaviour, attitudes, habits and thinking. How do we gauge their willingness to perform?

The willingness-ability, performance-potential grid will help determine the candidate's willingness and ability to perform.

Ability—what a candidate can do

Willingness—what a candidate is ready/willing to do

Performance—what a candidate does based on his/her ability and willingness

Potential—what the candidate can do based on the ability as well as willingness

	Performance	Potential
Ability	What an employee can do ➤ Knowledge & Education ➤ Skills ➤ Experience ➤ Degree of Proficiency	What s/he will be able to do ➤ Learning capacity ➤ Aptitude ➤ Intelligence ➤ Ambiguity management
Willingness	What s/he is willing to do ➤ Attitude ➤ Beliefs ➤ Values & Principles ➤ Personality	What s/he wants to do ➤ Career goals ➤ Interests & Motives

Adapted from Geof Lory's "Readiness: A Framework for Leadership"

Let us use examples to understand the concept better.

Example 1: With Annie's educational qualification, skills and experience she will be a good fit for the role. Recruiters can to a large extent judge her performance by comparing her performance in the previous organization, whereas, Annie's willingness can be determined by learning more about her attitude, values, beliefs and principles. i.e., if her attitude towards work is more inclined to wanting to get things done, quality, create better, etc., if the organization's values match hers and so on. Potential of the candidate is measured by focusing on the aptitude, how fast a learner she is, where her interest lies and if it correlates with the job role and so on.

Therefore, by following this structure, you will be able to gauge the candidate's willingness to perform.

Maximize Recruitment Effectiveness

Going back to what we spoke about in the first chapter, the competition out there is fierce, and we must be the best in what we do. What is it that makes your recruitment more effective than others? How can you remain on top of your game and be among the best organizations that recruit only the best?

- Be observant of what the market is like. Know how other organizations recruit their people. What are the other methods one can use to hire effectively?
- These are some of the questions that will allow you to stand out in the crowd.
- Build a network so that you have access to the best talent pool.
- Be self-motivated and curious in order to keep pace with the rapidly evolving talent landscape.

Constantly practising and developing positive habits are very important to become an effective recruiter.

DID YOU KNOW?

- There are now over 15 million brands and organizations available on Facebook. And it is interesting to note that over 18 million people found their job via Facebook.
- Over 10 million jobseekers found their job via LinkedIn. And 89% of recruiters have recruited someone via LinkedIn.

Chapter 8

Turning Challenges to Opportunities

What one often fails to realize is that hiring is a tedious task. Therefore, there are challenges that are bound to happen. Let us look at examples of challenges that can be faced by both the candidate and the interviewer.

While talking to a candidate about his first job interview, he revealed that he was ecstatic when he received his first interview call letter. He also mentioned that this was his first call back after sending out applications to 35 companies.

Reality is that this is the case with many prospective job seekers. Getting the right opportunity is not easy and requires a lot of hope, effort and patience. Let us listen to the problems he had to share.

Having read several books on how to send the right job application, how to attend an interview, etc., he managed to gather enough information that stimulates one's intellect, despite several bottlenecks that exist during the entire recruitment process. Irrespective of one's talent, qualifications and experience, good opportunities may not always come your way. Companies often complain that they're not getting the right talent and hence we have listed a few ways we can bridge this GAP that exists in the hiring process.

1. **Getting Your Application Noticed**: Job applications can get rejected from the Application Tracking System (ATS) by an employer. The reason as stated by them was that I didn't possess one of the criteria set by them. However, when I sent an InMail through LinkedIn to the Hiring Manager, I received

a call letter for the Personal Interview. The best part was that I got selected!!

In situations like these, do you blame the candidate or your hiring tools?

2. **Personal Interests**: The most unfair and unethical reason for your application getting rejected could be personal bias. There can be instances where the recruiter finds your gender, location, caste, etc. as inappropriate for the job profile.

Such an attitude is highly unprofessional and inappropriate for an interviewer to have.

3. **Large Number of Applicants:** In most cases, large companies invite applications for a job profile on several common platforms. This results in the large influx of job applications at one time. Candidates in these cases tend not to pay close attention to the job description and all these lead to your application getting lost in the heap of unwanted applications.

This is very common in case of MNC's where people tend to apply, solely based on the goodwill of the company. One should realize that too many cooks spoil the broth and, in this case, spoil the chance of getting an ideal candidate.

4. **Misconceptions**: This is one of the most common reasons for rejecting one's job application. A gap of three to six months in a candidate's job is often frowned upon. Another reason to get your resume declined is if they see you have worked at three places in the last six months. This makes you look like a "JOB HOPPER" thereby portraying you as non-committed and unreliable. There have been instances where a married woman has been denied a job stating her future obligations towards her family might get in the way of achieving company motives/goals.

Hypocrisy in hiring.

5. **Unscientific or Unhealthy Delay:** The time taken by the hiring managers to close a position is sometimes too big. Companies may mention "immediate requirement" on their job posting and it will take months to close it. The result is you might lose the right candidates. Similarly, when the recruiter calls you for an interview at 10:00 a.m. you are bound to be a responsible person and reach the venue 15 minutes earlier. However, there are instances where the candidates are made to wait for hours before the interviewee is called in, which is later owed to organizational emergency, meetings, department events, etc. Soon after, one representative comes and says, "Submit your resume, we will get back to you!" There is a change in the schedule due to an unforeseen meeting by the Hiring Manager!

I have been a victim to one or all of the above reasons and did not get selected by the interviewer or the Hiring Manager. All this made me terribly frustrated and completely demotivated me. I think every act of yours will have an impact on others' life; could be positive or negative. So be courteous!

Challenges Faced by an Interviewer

Manoj Pisharody, who has been recruiting candidates for corporates over a decade or so, says, "Whenever I am recruiting, I always look for the 'Need Factor'—whether the candidate really needs this job or not. This question usually comes to my mind before finalising a candidate. In my experience, a person will contribute and grow more, if he/she really needs the job. They will automatically acquire the skill set required to effectively function in their sphere of work. They will not be demotivated and will never complain about facilities or benefits provided.

I have faced many challenges in my recruiting career that are most commonly faced by every recruiter irrespective of industry or location. I even lost my job from one of my previous employers for not being able to close the positions on time. Now, you may think I am not a good recruiter. Quite obvious, misconceived minds! Please do not judge me based on my previous incident. You will find the reason from my explanations below."

1. **Lack of Plan**: "Manoj, we want ten Sales Executives to be hired immediately and they all should be on-board next week onwards".

   Your boss has no doubt on his requirement. Ok, I will, and I can! I then shortlisted a few candidates and lined them up for the interviews. HR shortlisted and forwarded to Sales Manager. Sales Manager found lack of energy, lack of knowledge, lack of skills based on the blind judgements. At last, the blame is on HR that they are not choosing the right candidates. HR must ensure the Subject Matter expertise of the candidate, Functional Skillsets of the candidates, Budget Negotiation with the candidates, Cultural Fit for the candidates, etc. during the interview.

2. **(Ir)Responsible Candidates**: You will see a lot of candidates for every position you may hire. When we call the candidates, they agree for the interview schedule and on the day, do not show up! Out of five candidates, three will face unforeseen hospitalization of their beloved ones. I am now afraid to call the candidates, as something will happen to their family members and have even started to ensure that the candidates I call for interview don't have grandparents! I had another experience where a candidate started from home early to attend the interview at 10:00 a.m. and did not reach the office till 4:00 p.m.! After that, his phone went dead and I really got anxious to know what had happened to him. Thankfully he was safe!!

   Casualty Department at HR!

3. **Lack of Objective**: After deep frustrations of applying for jobs and not getting hired, candidates become ready to do any job just to earn revenue to feed their family. They just start applying

blindly to any job and many of those may not even match their profiles. We find many such candidates during 'walk-in drives' or 'mass hiring' processes. It will ultimately end up in wasting our time and invite unwanted negativity.

Give me a job!

4. **Lack of Clarity**: HR will start the hiring process after getting the requirement from the department. Based on the requirement we shortlist and brief the candidates and when we send to the department heads, they share different stories and ultimately the candidates end up blaming the HR for wrong guidance.

    Recruiter Vs. HoDs – Heads of Department!

5. **Budget**: I think I am not the only person who has faced this challenge. You will find the best quality candidate but could not hire him/her because of budget constraints. The candidate may ask for a higher salary, but the company cannot afford the same. You will be surprised to know that budget constraints happen the other way also. The company might look for candidates from higher budgets for ensuring the right talents are paid well. But you will find the right candidates from lower budgets also because they did not get the right opportunities.

Habits of Highly Effective Recruiters

*   **Attune Yourself to the Changing Tide**: A growth mind-set and the ability to be open and welcome to changes are key features of highly adaptable recruiters.
*   **High Sense of Urgency and Efficiency**: As a recruiter, one should be able to develop and adhere to a schedule to increase productivity and effectiveness.
*   **Networking and Interpersonal Relationships:** If people with expertise in their area of work come together for the recruitment procedure, it would make the process easier and quicker. This would require effective communication and good interpersonal relationships.

- **Be Agile and Proactive:** In changing times, one must learn how to organize themselves and plan out their tasks according to the current requirement of the market.
- **Effective Planning and Prioritisation:** Learn to weed out the nonessential tasks from the pool of important tasks that require your immediate attention.

"If each of us hires people who are smaller than we are, we shall become a company of dwarfs. But if each of us hires people who are bigger than we are, we shall become a company of giants".

– David Ogilvy

Behaviour Response Exercise — CAPE

Below are some examples of responses given in an interview.

For each item, indicate which of the following elements are present by putting a ✔ in the appropriate column(s): Condition/Activity (C/A), Perform (P), Effect (E). If it is not a behavioural example, check NB.

Response	C/A	P	E	NB
1. I was involved in a project that focused on increasing student participation in the student union. We began with a survey to find out what students wanted from their union and why they were unsure of joining the union or how it can be pursued.				
2. An open meeting was held to understand concerns and find a way out. The project was well-received as we noticed an increase of 21% involvement in student participation.				
3. I was actively involved in many different activities that demanded my skills and knowledge of leadership.				

Continued...

Response	C/A	P	E	NB
4. There's an accident-prone, risky intersection near my office. I first went over to the police to understand the number of accidents that have occurred. Then I wrote a complaint explaining the problem in detail. I requested for a stop sign to be erected along with the speed breakers. I also got many volunteers to help me share the awareness among their friends and family, in the vicinity. We also campaigned with the drivers when they stopped at the office intersection.				
5. I also video-recorded the flow of speeding traffic at the office intersection with many risky situations and three serious accidents. The complaint along with the video evidence was discussed with the government officials of the town council. Now they have agreed to install a stop sign along with a speed breaker by the end of this month.				
6. During my days at school and college, I have always taken an active role in many activities. I was enrolled into many groups like Basketball Club, Boy Scouts, the Society for the Blind, the Red Cross Association, the Champions' Debate, the Campus Reading circle, Theatre and Drama Forum, First Aid Awareness Trainers, Green Campus Landscapers, Save Precious Water Campaign, Prevention of Cruelty to Animals and Freedom from Plastics Soldiers.				

Response	C/A	P	E	NB
7. It was my assignment in science, and I knew I was missing something vital. I spent the whole weekend with my textbooks and notes, figuring out what I could do different for the experiment to work. On Monday, I got into the science lab early and worked on my experiment and made necessary corrections. I was successful with positive outcomes.				
8. My proposal was that 'If you must do well in life, you must be proficient in English' in a global language programme among high school students. I divided the students based on their language proficiency, indicating that all people with poor English were inferior. I got the class to meet in their respective discussion forums for 20 minutes. They were told to ignore comments from those with poor English. The people shared their feelings when they reassembled.				
9. As a professional, to create something new is a way to realize myself in my profession as it allows me to generate new ideas and be busy with my practical experiments, get the results and keep fine-tuning through which I can reach the desired goal.				
10. I was always attracted to dance and wanted to learn from a good dance teacher. Since I could not afford the fees being a student myself, I found someone who was willing to barter lessons for some part-time data entry job. I've already learned a lot of dancing steps and passed several tests and continue to learn and practice every day.				

Continued...

Response	C/A	P	E	NB
11. My family and I planned an adventurous forest camping in the thick of the jungles and had booked a family cottage. Upon reaching there, I found that the floor of the cottage was wet due to seepage from the toilet. I got the resort staff to get it fixed. We enjoyed our holiday adventure.				
12. To make a difference in someone's life has been my wish all along. "You are good. You can do it" is a mentoring programme that I volunteered so that I can be of some help.				

Annexures

Fact Sheet for Psychometric Assessments
Benefit of FITS Personality Type

FITS Personality Type Assessment is based on the influences of one's heredity factors inherited through the parents since birth. The attitudes measured by the FITS assessment identify the true potential of the person in the given field. To unmask candidates, the knowledge of the genetic influences holds the key to understand the true potential of the candidate. This helps the best-fit dimensions for a given role and responsibility.

1. People with career happiness are those where the true potential is well supported right from the younger days as well as by the different environments in which they have lived or worked.

2. If the hidden potential is suppressed unknowingly and probably unintentionally, you will find lots of contradictions and confusion in the candidate's behaviour.

3. To gain happiness in career the secret is to align the environmental influences to support the heredity attitudes. One can witness a positive change.

   a. Name of the Assessment: FITS Personality Type

   b. Influence: Heredity (attitudes are embedded in the genetic coding and hence change from one to another is not likely to happen)

  c. Scope to Change FITS Behaviours: Negligible (Personality type can't change, but one's acceptance and resultant communication can change)

  d. Source: www.theassessmentworld.com

  e. Based on the Researcher: Carl Gustav Jung

  f. Language: English

  g. Field of Study: Psychology—Personality Types and Attitudes

  h. No. of Statements to Respond: 80

  i. Different Types of Personality:

    1. Feeler

    2. Intuitor

    3. Thinker

    4. Sensor

Brief Description of the Four Personality Types:

Feeler: Emotional, Friendly, Warm, Caring, Approachable, Talkative

Intuitor: Creative, Dreamer, Idea-driven, Futuristic, Looks for alternatives

Thinker: Logical, Analytical, Rational, Systematic, Sequential

Sensor: Action-driven, Result-oriented, Hands-on, Sense of urgency

Other Benefits of the FITS Personality Type Assessment:

- Self-awareness of one's strengths
- To find the right person for the right role
- Optimising one's true potential
- To bridge the gap between potential and current performance
- Develop the ability to flex one's communication style to get things done
- To get to know different people and use the right ways to get along with people

Benefit of 4C's Personality Style

4C's Personality Style Assessment is largely due to environmental influences in which one lives or works. It is heavily influenced by the upbringing dynamics in one's life along with the situational demands as faced by the individual. These nurturing influences on the candidate's behaviour, attitude and thinking can have a lasting impact, almost for a lifetime.

The 4C's inner motivational aspects help one to unmask the right person for the right role. The candidate's readiness for the given position or responsibility is relatively easier with these insights.

The differences between FITS Personality Type and 4C's Personality Style scores are suggestive of the gap between one's true potential and current performance. These two assessments together are valuable assets in unmasking candidates.

a. Name of the Assessment: 4C's Personality Style

b. Influence: Upbringing and Environmental (Impact of Conditioned Behaviours are long-lasting and hence not easy to change)

c. Scope to Change 4C's Behaviours: Difficult but possible with effort

d. Source: www.theassessmentworld.com

e. Based on the Researcher: William Moulton Marston

f. Language: English

g. Field of Study: Psychology – Personality Styles and Inner Motivations

h. No. of Statements to Respond: 64

i. Different Styles of Personality:

   1. **Controlling**—Authoritative, Strong-willed, Goal-driven, Competitive

   2. **Convincing**—Persuasive, Approachable, Charming, Friendly

3. **Conforming**—Planner, Methodical, Organized, Detail-oriented

4. **Consistent**—Harmonious, Subject Matter specialist, Team player, Diplomatic

Other Benefits of the 4C's Personality Style Assessment:

- Knowledge of one's strengths
- To get the right person for the right role
- Maximising one's hidden capabilities and competence
- To minimise the gap between one's true capability and existing performance
- Identifying one's inner drives and motivations
- Get the best out one's life and career
- To understand people differences
- Learn to flex one's communication style in dealing with different people and situations for optimum results

Benefit of PPC 20 (People Performance Competency)

Capability and competency are critical factors in unmasking candidates to gauge their ability to live up to the role expectations. Every role demands a set of competencies from the candidate and every candidate has developed a set of competencies. The unmasking is all about finding the right fit between what the role demands versus what the candidate possesses. PPC 20 measures the strength of the candidate in 20 generic current competencies. In a way, PPC 20 provides insight on the extent of readiness of the candidate in performing to live up to the demands of the job.

FITS Personality Type measures the natural potential for developing different competencies. 4C's Personality Style measures the impact of nurturing on developing the said competencies. PPC 20 measures the current state of mind of the candidate in terms of the efforts made by flowering of the strengths of the nature and nurturing in one's life and career thus far. It is the level of application by the candidate and not just the potential or hidden talent.

a. Name of the Assessment: PPC 20 People Performance Competency 20

b. Influence: Situational demands and Environmental necessities

c. Scope to Change PPC 20 Behaviours: Possible with effort

d. Source: www.theassessmentworld.com

e. Based on the Researchers: Richard Boyatzis, David McClelland, Kirton, Mintzberg

f. Language: English

g. Field of Study: Psychology—Behavioural Competency

h. No. of Statements to Respond: 160

i. 5 Meta Performance Competencies and 20 traits:

Managing Change—Initiative, Risk Taking, Innovation and Flexibility/Adaptability

Planning and Organising—Analytical Thinking, Decision Making, Planning and Quality Focus

Interpersonal Relations—Oral Communication, Sensitivity, Relationships and Teamwork

Result Orientation—Achievement, Customer Focus, Business Awareness and Learning Orientation

Leadership—Authority/Presence, Motivating People, Developing People and Resilience

More Benefits of PPC 20:

Quantifying the candidates' performance competencies helps in recognising their strengths and limitations. Measuring where they stand on a specific skill or ability with respect to their roles and responsibilities would help identify gaps. This helps determine a candidate's job-fit for the given role. PPC 20 considers the negative and positive implications of each score, be it Minimal, Ideal or Over-Strength (Uncharacteristically High).

Benefit of CPA (Communication Pattern Analysis)

Communication is the essence of enabling and empowering interpersonal dynamics in any organization. Cooperation, coordination, or collaboration depends on one's ability to communicate effectively. Unknowingly and unintentionally, people develop communication patterns that they are comfortable with. The CPA—Communication Pattern Analysis brings out the effectiveness or the ineffectiveness of the candidate's communication. It helps you unmask the candidate's Theory 'X' or Theory 'Y' behaviour. You will know what to expect and what not to expect in one's day to day communication.

The good thing is that these communication patterns are extensively influenced by both genetic as well as upbringing or environmental conditioning. The candidate's patterns of communication could be driven by nature or by nurturing influences. The patterns of communication as researched by Eric Berne in Transactional Analysis demonstrates strong influences of all three—the personality types, styles as well as the competency traits.

- a. Name of the Assessment: CPA—Communication Pattern Analysis
- b. Influence: Environmental
- c. Scope to Change CPA Behaviours: Possible with effort
- d. Source: www.theassessmentworld.com
- e. Based on the Researcher: Eric Berne, Douglas McGregor
- f. Language: English
- g. Field of Study: Psychology—Transactional Analysis
- h. No. of Statements to Respond: 60
- i. Different attributes of Communication Patterns:
    1. Advising
    2. Criticising
    3. Empathising
    4. Searching (Probing)

Other Benefits of the CPA—Communication Pattern Analysis Assessment:

Awareness of what to expect and what not to expect from the candidate is the key to making a solid decision on hiring. The patterns of communication one gets to experience from the candidate are clues to ascertain the suitability for a given job role and responsibility. Since the patterns are driven largely by environmental influences, one can work to change or improve one's pattern. But awareness of the same is the key aspect to bring about positive changes instrumental in helping people build interpersonal relationships and to influence them favourably to achieve the given objectives.

Benefit of BPA (Behavioural Pattern Analysis)

BPA – Behavioural Pattern Analysis measures the key influences of 'Situational Dynamics' in the candidate's life and career. The school, home, work or neighbourhood environments rarely change drastically and hence have a 'Conditioning Influence' on one's behaviour due to constant exposure to similar environmental pattern repetitions. Over a period of regular exposure to such repetitive environments, one develops a conditioned mind-set. This mind-set can be positive or negative. While unmasking candidates, it is essential to understand one's behavioural patterns at-work or off-work to gain insights into their performance expectations in given roles and responsibilities.

Even though BPA measures the conditioned situational behaviours, one can easily establish a clear linkage between the genetic types, upbringing styles, nurtured competencies, and communication patterns.

    a. Name of the Assessment: BPA—Behavioural Pattern Analysis

    b. Influence: Environmental

    c. Scope to Change BPA Behaviours: Possible with effort

    d. Source: www.theassessmentworld.com

    e. Based on the Researcher: B.F.Skinner

    f. Language: English

g. Field of Study: Psychology—Situational Dynamics

h. No. of Statements to Respond: 64

i. Different attributes of Behavioural Patterns:

1. Diplomatic versus Outspoken (Communication Style)

2. Introvert versus Extrovert (Interpersonal Relations)

3. High Versus Low (Sense of Urgency)

4. Innovative versus Systematic (Information Processing)

Other Benefits of the BPA – Behaviour Pattern Analysis Assessment:

Helps understand the candidate's behaviour across work and off-work situations. The candidate's behaviour is influenced by the environment in which one has lived or worked. Long-term exposure to different cultures, attitudes, emotions, values, ethics, authority, rapport, persuasion, coercion and/or genetics has its impact on the candidates' behaviour. BPA brings to light the manner of behaviours across varying situations. Hence you will have a balanced view of the likely behaviours, attitudes and thought processes of the candidate. It provides realistic insights that help make up your mind in getting the right person for the right job.

Benefits of LEAP (Leadership Effectiveness Aptitude Profile)

Leadership effectiveness is a critical success factor in many important roles and responsibilities across the organization at various levels of hierarchy. The LEAP assessment brings out the different leadership styles of the candidate. LEAP brings to light, the personal leadership style of the candidate and its implications in one's ability to flex one's style to suit the situational demand. LEAP enables you to know if the candidate leads one's team by defining goals and organizing systems and resources to minimize wastages and maximize profitability. LEAP also assesses if the candidate actively provides feedback in developing people, leads by providing a vision for the future or by example and personal experience in the chosen field of expertise.

a. Name of the Assessment: LEAP—Leadership Effectiveness Aptitude Profile

b. Influence: Environmental

c. Scope to Change LEAP Behaviours: Possible with effort

d. Source: www.theassessmentworld.com

e. Based on the Researcher(s): Peter Drucker, James McGregor Burns, Paul Hersey, Ken Blanchard, Robert House

f. Language: English

g. Field of Study: Psychology—Situational Dynamics

h. No. of Statements to Respond: 48

i. Different attributes of LEAP Assessment:

   1. Organizer—Systems Driven Style

   2. Coach—People-Person Style

   3. Entrepreneur—The Visionary Style

   4. Specialist—Technical Expert Style

Other Benefits of the LEAP—Leadership Effectiveness Aptitude Profile:

All four styles are present to a greater or lesser degree in each of the candidates, shaped by their heredity and environment. LEAP assessment is an objective tool that identifies the candidate's leadership style and quantifies the same. It is a scientific self-searching leadership tool that serves as a neutral means of strengthening one's leadership strength. The idea is to choose the right leader for the right role in the given situation. LEAP throws light on what can the candidate do or is able to do by learning and development. LEAP uncovers the willingness beyond just what the candidate wants.

SAMPLE OF BEHAVIOUR-BASED INTERVIEW QUESTIONS

Behaviour-based interviewing helps you interviewers identify behaviours of the candidates by using certain types of questions. Here are a few job-related open-ended questions that will help you in assessing the behaviours and skills of the candidate in ten different dimensions.

Dimension: Time Distribution	
The optimum use of time to maximize the results of self and others	
Sl. No.	Behaviour-Based Questions
1	Explain about any one situation where you were the team/project leader and the task was not completed on time. How did you deal with this issue?
2	Is there any current project(s) you are working on? If so, describe how you have planned your time for each.
3	Was there any situation where your manager gave you conflicting tasks/projects? If so, how did you deal with it?
4	If you know that a project you are working on is going to miss the deadline, how would you ensure to get it back on track?
5	How many hours a day do you typically work and how much time do you take to do a particular task? (it can be any; use one example).
6	Describe how a typical workday looks like for you.
7	How do you plan and prioritize your work when there is a lot of work in hand?

Dimension: Risk Taking	
Views failure as an opportunity for growth despite personal risk or exposure	
Sl. No.	Behaviour-Based Questions
1	Would you take risks or play it safe? If so, describe a situation that supports the same.
2	Describe a situation where you were not supported in a task and how you dealt with it.
3	Do you think of yourself as taking ownership, accountability and responsibility for your work as well as your team's performance?
4	How do you determine if a task/project is worth taking a risk for?
5	What do you think of the phrase, "no risk, no reward"?

6	How do you encourage your team to take risks?
7	If your stakeholders do not support your decision of going ahead with a particular project (with high risk), would you still go ahead and do it? How will you manage the situation and the project?
8	How do you decide if something is risky?
9	Do you weigh the pros and cons before jumping into conclusions? Describe one instance the supports the same.
10	What according to you is "calculated risk"?

Dimension: Learning Agility/Growth Mind-set

The ability to absorb and adapt new learning to the existing environment.

Sl. No.	Behaviour-Based Questions
1	Have you ever been a part of any behavioural training at your workplace? If so, how has it helped you both in your personal and professional life?
2	What are the new things you have learned after having joined your previous jobs?
3	How has this new learning helped you?
4	Have you taken initiatives to learn something new? If so, what was it?
5	What is the biggest challenge you have faced at your workplace with respect to lack of knowledge?
6	How did you deal with this challenge?
7	What are your strengths and weaknesses? How do you plan to overcome your weaknesses?

Dimension: Decision Making

Ability to make a timely/quality decision not necessarily with all the information needed.

Sl. No.	Behaviour-Based Questions
1	How do you usually take decisions? Is there a process you follow? Describe.
2	What are the external factors you consider before making a decision?

Continued...

3	Describe a situation where you had to get your stakeholders to agree with you on a particular decision?
4	What is the one decision you made you are extremely proud of (personal/professional) and why?
5	Do you ask for others' opinions before you make decisions?
6	Describe a decision you regret. How did you handle the situation?
7	Describe a situation where you had 2/3 viable options to choose from to reach your goal and how you made the decision.
8	Do you usually make your own decision or agree on the decision you think is apt? Can you explain it with an instance?

Dimension: Leadership	
Demonstrating by example, the willingness to be out in front.	
Sl. No	**Behaviour-Based Questions**
1	What are the qualities you think a leader should possess?
2	What are the methods you adopt to mentor your team?
3	What are the feedbacks you have received from your stakeholders regarding your leadership skills?
4	Do you agree to the statement leaders don't do different things, but they do it differently? If so, why?
5	Describe a situation where you had put this statement into practice. (personal/professional).
6	What do you think is the role of the organization in making leaders?
7	What is it that makes you different from other leaders? (Or) Why do you think you can be a better leader?
8	How can you make yourself to be a better leader?

\multicolumn{2}{c	}{**Dimension: Interpersonal Relationship**}
\multicolumn{2}{c	}{*Ability to relate/communicate/empathize with all organizational levels*}
Sl.no	**Behaviour-Based Questions**
1	What was the biggest challenge you faced in your workplace with respect to getting along with others?
2	How much time do you usually take to get along with others?
3	How important is it for you to be perceived as a team member and why?
4	What efforts do you take to be seen as a team player?
5	What according to you are your strengths in terms of interpersonal skills?
6	From your experience who was the easiest to work with and why?
7	Which kind of people do you find difficult to work with?
8	Describe the relationship you maintain with various types of your stakeholders.
9	Describe a conflict situation you have been a part of and how did you handle it?

\multicolumn{2}{c	}{**Dimension: Communication skills**}
\multicolumn{2}{c	}{*Ability to influence or present ideas logically through verbalization.*}
Sl. No	**Behaviour-Based Questions**
1	Do you often find it difficult to put across your point of view to other stakeholders? Describe a situation.
2	How large was the largest audience you presented to?
3	What do you think are your developmental areas when it comes to improving your oral communication?
4	Have you ever been uncomfortable in front of a group? Why?
5	Describe the best presentation you ever gave and why you think it went so well.
6	Describe a situation where you felt you were being misunderstood and that give rise to a conflict. How did you handle it?

Continued...

| 7 | What is your method of building rapport with others? |
| 8 | Describe a time where you had to put across a piece of sensitive information to a team member. How did you do it? |

Dimension: Change Agility	
Views and welcomes change as necessary for people and organizational growth.	
Sl. No	Behaviour-Based Questions
1	Describe one instance where you bought about a positive change in your team/organization.
2	In your work experience, what was the most challenging change? And why was it challenging?
3	How do you motivate your team members to adapt to new and changing environments?
5	What according to you needs to change in today's workplace? And why?
6	How do you implement these changes?
7	Do you believe in "challenging the status quo"? Why?

Identifying the Winning Candidate's Profile:

- **Set Your Eyes on the Goal:** One needs to align their short-term and long-term goals of the candidate with that of the organization. To do so, it is imperative to know whether the candidate has completed the task that was already assigned to him.

- **Planning and Prioritising:** A candidate must be able to prioritize his/her work keeping the future in mind. An ideal candidate achieves the goal using a set of methods that are clear, disciplined and intelligent.

- **Taking Charge:** Is the candidate an active initiator or a passive responder? Does he wait for others to lead and enjoys following?

- **Interpersonal Skills and Communication:** An ideal candidate will reflect the traits of a team player more than an individual contributor. Also, he/she should be willing to maintain already existing relationships through effective communication and should be able to convey the right message across.

- **Leadership:** As a leader, one should be able to display a certain amount of confidence and should be capable of influencing others and leading the team to achieve organizational goals.

- **Eagerness:** An ideal candidate must be able to enthuse himself and his team members. His way of communication should reflect that he's a vibrant and energetic individual. He/she should be an active initiator rather than a passive responder to people and situations around him.

- **Drive:** The candidate must be able to strive for the best result rather than settling for the average.

- **Resilience:** The candidate must have the ability to revive himself after a failure or setback. He/she should be ready to learn from mistakes instead of taking matters to heart.

Authors Bio

The authors of the book, *Unmasking Candidates*, are a team of behavioural experts who ardently believe in bringing out the hidden behaviours, attitude and thinking of individuals.

Both Mr. Sreenidhi S.K and Ms. Tay Chinyi Helena are directors of Oscar Murphy Life Strategists, with tonnes of experience in the corporate, especially recruitment as well as academic world. As Life Strategists and change catalysts, they have enabled thousands of individuals to live happy lives and have productive careers. They have energized business leaders, entrepreneurs and organizations.

Ms. Anjali S. Nair and Ms. Feby S. John specialized in Counselling Psychology and Political Science respectively, have been the backbone in supporting a vast magnitude of global clientele. The team has helped people from all walks of life to develop their key competencies to enable strategic thinking and lead purposeful lives with utmost satisfaction and happiness.

www.ingramcontent.com/pod-product-compliance
Lightning Source LLC
Chambersburg PA
CBHW021420210526
45463CB00001B/465